GROWING PAYNES

A Lifetime Journey from
Adversity to Happiness

William Theodore Payne

ISBN: 9798615823916

Published by William T. Payne
P.O. Box 21225, Chattanooga, TN 37424

Dedication

I would like to dedicate this book to every Yooper — past, present, and future. If you have visited the Upper Peninsula of Michigan, you know Yoopers to be friendly and welcoming people…
and they are my people.

"It is one of the prettiest places in the world."
Henry Ford, in the 1920s

Contents

Introduction

A LOT OF PEOPLE HAVE written a book about their lives, and I imagine there are millions more who have considered it. What might stop many people from writing a book is that it is really hard to begin to make it happen. It involves a lot of detail and winds up being a large investment of time and money, which makes it easy to put off.

Then the speculation aspect can stop people: *Will other people think my life is interesting enough to want to buy my book, if and when I do write it?* In a lot of respects, writing a book is like writing a song. A songwriter and an author have much in common. A songwriter doesn't know if their song is going to be a hit until they get it out there and it has good exposure. The same applies to an author. Acceptance by the general public is certainly not a given.

Hi, folks. My name is William Theodore Payne, and if life were a game, I would be in the fourth quarter. To be honest, I might be in overtime. I have done some writing in my lifetime, but just for a hobby. I have written some poems and short stories, but this is my first book.

I have a story to tell that will encourage people going through tough times, especially children from broken homes. I want people to see that a child can go through devastation and total unhappiness without many people noticing or understanding their situation.

It is important to me to show this through the eyes of a child. Most children will not confide in adults about their innermost feelings. When they are older, and look back, they may be able to talk about and perhaps understand them. That is not to say that all children are willing to talk about their feelings when they become adults. Some do not, even though they might want to. I hope, in this book, that I speak for them also.

Another reason I wanted to write this book was to perhaps help people more fully understand our great country of the United States of America. Yes, I understand we have a lot of problems we didn't have in the past, and there is unrest and dissension in a greater proportion than ever before. But through it all, we are still the Land of Opportunity.

I hope that even though you may feel handicapped due to lack of education or money, you can rise above these conditions through hard work and dedication, and be successful and happy. I hope to help others follow their dreams and achieve them if they are willing to sacrifice and work hard. The opportunity is there, just waiting for dedicated, hardworking people to find.

A song comes to mind that applies to my life, except I have to stop in midstream and change the lyrics a bit: *I've lived a life that's full, I've traveled each and every highway, But more, much more than this...* I DID NOT do it my way. The decisions I made in my life and the things I have done were not always my preference or my way. A good portion of the decisions were based on family needs or circumstances beyond my control; but most importantly they were based on a love, respect, and trust that I have in the living God.

In today's politically correct society, it is not popular to say that you are a Christian. I need to be perfectly honest in that regard because my trust in God is what carried me through some very, very tough times. I made a lot of mistakes and did some things that I should not have done, but to me, saying that you are a Christian is really just admitting you are a sinner and need help.

I have been in and out of church several times during my life, so I know the flip side of the coin. I have done my share of partying and drinking, although I am not proud of that fact. I gave thought to how much of that portion of my life I should put in this book. It would not be honest to say that a lot of these actions were not fun — they were. There is fun in going out, drinking, being with your friends, and cutting up. The problem is that it can have severe side effects. In my case, some were severe enough to cause me to shy away from the all-out party times I was involved in. Please understand that I do not condemn anyone for their lifestyle. I am just stating what works and does not work in my life.

The final decision to write my life story came because of the encouragement and support of my Facebook friends. I posted a chapter or two online to see how it was received. The response was overwhelming. I cannot even count how many people suggested that I write a book. The one or two chapters that I initially posted wound up being a whole lot more. People constantly encouraged me to write. They would go into detail about why they liked my writings, and finally, after thinking about it for years, I decided to go with it. I reasoned that if they liked it, maybe others will, too.

I was especially impressed with the support I received from what I call my home base. These are people in the Upper Peninsula of Michigan, in cities like Ironwood — where I was raised — and Bessemer, and Wakefield. I have felt a deep kinship with the people in this area. Even though I do not know many of them personally, I feel like we have much in common that binds us together.

We shared the climate, which included tons of snow. We shared some of the same schools, workplaces, and trades, such as mining and logging. We shared a dish called "pasties" that is unique to the area. Joe's Pasty shop in downtown Ironwood is still in business after opening in 1946, and most of us stop there every time we go back home for a visit.

When people ask me where I am from, I always reply, "The Upper Peninsula (UP) of Michigan, from a small city called Iron-wood." Many people confuse Ironwood with Iron Mountain, which is located toward the eastern end of the UP. Ironwood is on the far western border and is a twin city with Hurley, Wisconsin. They are separated by the Montreal River.

It is a beautiful area. There is usually plenty of snow for winter outdoor sports like skiing, snowboarding, and snowmobiling. The summers are nice and cool the majority of the time, and the fall colors would rival any state for beauty.

A word that refers to people from the UP has come into usage in my lifetime. We are called "Yoopers." We are proud of the fact that we are now defined by that one word. I am sure many people in the eastern and western states have never heard of the word, but it is an endearing term in this part of the country.

In trying to come up with a title for this book, I decided to ask my Facebook friends for suggestions. There was a great response and some really good titles were suggested, making it extremely difficult to choose one. I had a total of thirty suggested titles, so I posted them and let everyone vote. Then I took the top five vote-getters and posted those. After that, I took the final two and asked for a vote. Would you believe the vote was sixty-nine for one and sixty-nine for the other? A tie!

After agonizing over it, I went with the one that I thought was the better of the two, and this resulted in the title being *GROWING PAYNES*. A big thank you to Adam Kangas for submitting that title. I also want to thank all of my friends who participated in the process.

I determined in writing my memoirs that I was going to be as honest about my feelings as possible. I decided not to hold back, even though some of my thoughts are embarrassing, hurtful, and very painful. In parts of this book, I had to stop for a period of time to compose myself, as my emotions would get the best of me. There were parts I decided to skip because they were too difficult to relate, but then I would go back and write them anyway.

I have had so much drama in my life that as I was writing I would think, *Maybe too much drama can be boring!* But then, this is the story of my life, and I do not want to use speculation or other rea-soning to leave out parts. We all realize there is no way to cram an entire lifetime into a two-hundred (or so) page book and not leave out some things. But I cannot leave out the highlights and the very emotional times, even though they are hard to write about.

And so, dear reader, I invite you to come along with me on this journey. It is the journey of my lifetime with all of its ups and downs. A journey plagued with bad memories as well as many good memories. It has been a lonely journey to a certain extent, and it is a journey that is almost over. Writing about my life is like taking the journey over again. However, this time it is more com-forting because I know you are along with me for the ride.

My Family Tree

Mother's Side

Mother Mary -1916	Aunt Sadie -1918	Uncle Joseph -1920
Rosemary (Dolly) 1932	Kathleen (Kathy)	James (Jimmy)
Raymond (Ray) 1941	Charmaine	Joseph (Joey)
William (Billy) 1942		Robert (Bobby)
Barbara (Barb) 1947		
John (Johnny) 1949		
Ronald (Ronnie) 1951		

William (Bill) Payne -1942

Charles Theodore (Ted) 1961
William Timothy (Tim) 1964
Angela Renee (Angie) 1975

L—R: Grandma Gallo, Charmaine (Aunt Sadie's daughter), Bill, Bobby (Uncle Joe's son), Ray, Jean (Ray's wife), Aunt Sadie

Ironwood, Michigan — where I was raised

1 The Very Early Years

MY GRANDMOTHER, ROSE MONTIPERTO, CAME to America from Sicily at the age of fourteen. My grandfather, James Gallo, came at about the same time, and they each settled in an Italian neighborhood on the south side of Chicago, where they met and later married. We affectionately referred to them as Grandpa and Grandma Gallo.

They lived in the same neighborhood as Al Capone, the famous South Side Chicago gangster. It is hard to believe, but the community really loved Al Capone. He did a lot for the people in their eyes, but then again these were not the eyes of the many people he had killed.

Grandpa and Grandma had three children. My mother, Mary, was the oldest and was born in 1916. Aunt Sadie was next, born in 1918, followed by my Uncle Joe, born in 1920.

I am not sure what Grandpa did for a living, but Grandma was a seamstress for a furrier company in Chicago. This was back in the days when real fur was very popular, especially mink. Grandma did piecework; she was paid a fixed price per piece of work done. When the children were old enough to help, she brought work home and had them all help. Mink collars on dress coats were popular, and Grandma did a lot of that type of work.

She worked hard and was very thrifty with her money. By the time I was born, Grandma already owned a 3-flat building located at 6058 S. Massasoit Avenue, Chicago, Illinois. There were no ZIP codes back then. A flat was the common name used for a one-level apartment that was primarily rented by the working class.

During the Great Depression when the bottom fell out of the real estate market and many people were losing their houses, Grandma bought quite a few of them very cheaply and rented them out. Later, she teamed up with a carpenter and they started remodeling them. As soon as they finished remodeling one building, she would sell it and move on to the next one. I do not know how many she had, but I was told that it was a lot.

Typical 3-flat in Chicago

Many in the family, including us, lived in the 3-flat where I was born. I always looked up to Grandma Gallo because she came from a foreign country with a limited education, and through hard work and discipline, became a very successful business woman.

I don't know who took care of Mary, Sadie, and Joe when they were small and while Grandma was working, but my guess is someone on Grandma's side of the family helped, as her brother and sister had come from Sicily and lived close by. Grandpa also had a brother and sister in America, so my mother had many cousins to relate to while she was growing up.

When my mother Mary was ten years old, she began taking care of Aunt Sadie and Uncle Joe during the summer months. Grandma worked long hours and Grandpa would come home and help with the cooking, but not every night. He would often stay out drinking with his friends. It's easy to conclude that my mother did not have much time for a social life. Since there was no adult supervision available during the day, the cousins would frequently come over to visit and would sometimes bring their friends.

14

Aunt Sadie, Bill, Grandma Gallo, Uncle Joe — mid-1970s

My mother was fifteen years old when it was discovered that she was pregnant. In those days, if a man impregnated a woman, the only honorable thing to do was to marry her. Her boyfriend was also Italian. And in the culture back then, it was a no-brainer—he would have to marry her, and so he did.

On July 3, 1932, my sister Rosemary (Dolly) was born. My mother had turned sixteen and was a very, very young mother. It became obvious that her husband did not want to stay married, so when Dolly was young, he deserted his family and moved to New York. He never returned to Chicago.

Grandma Payne, Dolly, Mother, Billy

I am not sure how old Dolly was when her dad left, but she was too young to remember him. To my knowledge, my mother never pressed him for child support. Thankfully, Mother was not alone. She lived with her mother, Grandma Gallo, and was surrounded by family. I feel comfortable in saying that Dolly never went hungry.

Dolly never saw her father again. In fact, nobody in the family saw him, except for Uncle Joe. Many years later, Uncle Joe looked him up in New York and took him out to dinner. He was remarried and had a family of his own, but he never told his new wife about Dolly. It was pretty obvious that he did not want anything to do with her at this point. I had many conversations with Dolly over the years. This act of total neglect by her father haunted her for the rest of her life.

After the divorce, my mother remained single for approximately six years, fulfilling her role as a single parent. Then in 1940, Mother met and married Lester Lawrence Payne, who would become my father several years later.

One of my mother's favorite cousins was Jimmy Granna, the son of Grandma Gallo's sister. They were close to the same age and had grown up together since Jimmy's family lived in the same 3-flat as my mother's family. I heard years later that they were as close as any brother and sister could be. If Mother had a problem, she could talk to Jimmy about it, and the reverse was also true.

Jimmy met a woman named Mary — same first name as my mother — whose ex-boyfriend had deserted her as soon as he found out she was pregnant. Mother could well relate to that situation as she was also deserted. Jimmy and Mary started dating and fell in love. The baby was born about the time Jimmy and Mary started going together. For whatever reason, they immediately brought the baby to my mother to take care of.

It would only be speculation on my part as to why they did not or could not keep the baby, but on February 10, 1942, my father and mother adopted baby Ray, who was almost four months old. And so baby Ray became Raymond Leslie Payne. My father also adopted Dolly at the same time and changed her name from Rosemary Gallo to Rosemary Payne. Ironically, my mother was six months pregnant with yours truly on the day of their adoption. Thus, when I was born on May 9, 1942, I had a six-month-old brother Ray, and a nine-year-old sister Dolly.

Father Lester Payne, Mother, brother Ray

I was born at Englewood Hospital in Chicago, Illinois, with the given name of William Theodore Payne. My mother was twenty-six, and my father was thirty-three years old, on that date.

It was a tumultuous time in history. The Japanese had bombed Pearl Harbor five months prior to my birth, and World War II was raging. The war was a global conflict that lasted from 1939 to 1945. At this time women flocked to the factories and other workplaces.

There was a shortage of men to work in these industries because so many of them went into the Armed Forces in defense of our country, either being drafted or enlisting.

Many children did not have a father figure in their home during World War II because so many men were in the service of our country. Married men with children were even drafted, and many grandmothers assumed control of their grandchildren when their daughters entered the workforce. Manufacturing soared with the demand for war materials, and certain foods and commodities were rationed during the war.

Mother with Billy

When I was born, my father worked at the Inland Glass Co., which manufactured glass for the war effort. This exempted him from the draft. My mother was listed on my birth certificate as a housewife. I am not sure what year it was, but my mother and Aunt Sadie worked at the same glass factory for a while. I have seen pictures of them at their place of employment when they were having some type of employee's party.

Patriotism was at an all-time high, and the country was united behind the war effort. The American serviceman was put on a pedestal during World War II because it was a just war — the enemy had attacked, and we retaliated. We achieved our goal and the war ended with us and our allies being victorious. This was the generation that the famous news commentator, Tom Brokaw, referred to as the Greatest

Father Lester Payne with Ray, Dolly with Billy

Generation. There has never been a war since then that had Americans as united as they were in World War II.

When I was born, our entire family still lived in the 3-flat on Massasoit Avenue in Chicago. This included our immediate family, and Uncle Joe and Aunt Sadie's families also. Many, many years later, Uncle Joe drove me by the building to show me where we all had lived. He was overwhelmed with emotion as it brought back the memories. In many family gatherings through the years, it was

Uncle Joe's son Jimmy and Bill — 1980s

always referred to as "the house on Massasoit." It seemed like most of our relatives lived there at one time or another, and the building is still there.

Since I have to reach way back in my memory bank, I naturally draw some blanks in my first few years. I know that our family moved from Massasoit Avenue to a home of our own, somewhere in the south side of Chicago. I remember a couple of dramatic events that happened when I was three years old, or perhaps closer to four years. The details are a little sketchy, but my sister Dolly helped fill in some of the blanks for me.

Ray and Billy

Ray and I were playing outside and chased a dog across the street. I bolted into the street and was struck by a car. Dolly was watching us and later told me there was no way she could have stopped me because of how quickly the event took place. Fortunately, the driver of the car had slammed on his brakes and did not hit me as hard as it appeared. The car knocked me down, and I had some skinned areas on my face and arms. However, I had banged my head hard enough to be unconscious for a few minutes.

Dolly told me that the driver, a man by himself, jumped out of the car and ran to where I was lying down. When he saw me, he went into hysterics thinking he might have killed me. Mother came running out of the house, sobbing when she came to my side. The hysterical man calmed down when he saw me stand up, and apologized profusely. It turned out that I was fine and had no broken bones, just some scrapes and scratches, and a big knot on my head.

One day Ray and I were swinging on a set of swings in our back yard, and my mother had started a fire close by to burn some trash. There were no strict burning rules back then. Mother had lit the fire and told us to be sure to stay away from it, as she was going back into the house.

Yeah, right! As soon as she went inside, we began to investigate the fire. Using the reasoning power of four-year-olds, we decided

18

to see if we could jump over the fire without getting burned. Ray went first, with a running start, and he jumped over the fire. I was not to be outdone, so I got a running start and jumped. And, yes, I did not clear the fire but landed right in the center of it. The left leg of my pants caught fire and immediately began to blaze.

I suppose we all know what to do if our pants are on fire, right? Instinct took over and I did what I thought I should do, and that was to run to the house, screaming for Mama. I ran screaming up the steps to the back porch. She opened the door, grabbed me, and started beating out the fire with her bare hands. She finally managed to just jerk my pants off and put out the fire.

The inside of my left leg was severely burned from the knee almost to the ankle. I remember her cracking eggs into a bowl and rubbing the liquid on my leg. Hmmm! I have never heard of that as a treatment for a burn, but I guess mothers know best. She took me to the hospital, or maybe a doctor's office, for treatment. When we left the center, my left leg was bandaged from my knee to my ankle. My mother had burned her hands, and both of them were bandaged.

You have heard many stories, as have I, about a mother's love. A lot of flowery words are used to describe it, especially around Mother's Day. And they are deserving, for sure. However, I am going to make a statement that may not be lovely sounding, but best depicts my mother's love during this incident: *A mother's love is intense.*

Mother, Ray, and Billy

The next part of my story is going to be extremely hard for me, but I had vowed before starting this book to be as honest as I could be and not hold back. I loved my mother very much. Sometime after the war ended in 1945, she met John Spetz, who was from Ironwood, Michigan, and who had been recently discharged from the Army. John had a sister, Sonja, who lived in Elmhurst, Illinois, and he decided to live with her after the war ended and perhaps get a job in the Chicago area.

I do not know how or when they started having the affair that led to my father and mother getting a divorce and Mother marrying John Spetz. The worst thing about this divorce was the custody battle over Dolly, Ray and me. The court awarded custody of yours truly to my father and custody of Dolly and Ray to my mother.

Why do courts separate children in a family? I did not want to live with my father. I wanted to stay with my mother, Ray, and Dolly. I imagine the fact that my father had done nothing wrong, and my mother was at fault, had something to do with it. Perhaps that seemed the right and fair thing to do. I didn't care about it being fair — I wanted my mother, brother, and sister.

Father was a strict disciplinarian. Although I believe he loved me, I did not love him nearly as much as my mother. It just didn't seem right for the court to separate a child from their mother and siblings. At the time, my father had moved in with his mother and that was where I would be staying.

Grandma Payne was a strict and proper English lady with a heavy emphasis on manners and being very proper. I was used to my Italian family who were much warmer and more affectionate.

Billy and Ray in uniform

I started resenting my father because I blamed him for the loss of my mother, Ray, and Dolly. I was not old enough to have compassion for my father, who had just lost most of his family over his wife's adulterous affair, where he was not at fault. I am sure he went through hell over this. I guess I was the consolation prize, and I didn't like it one little bit.

My Grandma Gallo had become a Seventh Day Adventist (SDA) when she moved to America. Thus, my mother was raised SDA, and she went to the church school all of her young life. When my father and mother were married, my father converted to Adventism, and we would all go to church every week. After moving in with my father and Grandma Payne, this practice continued, only it was just my father and I going to church. Grandma Payne was a very strict Catholic and did not like her son belonging to an Adventist Church, Naturally, she never went to church with us.

Mother, John, Ray, and Dolly still lived in the Chicago area, but I don't know how far away they were from us. I remember going to bed at night feeling so unhappy and sometimes crying. I missed my mother so much, and also Ray and Dolly. My mother was awarded visitation rights, but it was only on the weekend and she was always by herself. I don't know why Dolly and Ray were not allowed to come with her. I also was not allowed to leave with her to go anywhere. I would spend some time alone with her in one of the rooms and sometimes outside. She would always hug and kiss me and say that she loved me. When she started to leave, I would go ballistic and start crying uncontrollably. I wanted to go with her.

I don't remember exactly how long I lived with my father and Grandma Payne, but it doesn't seem like it was very long before something dramatic happened.

My father and I always walked to church. One Saturday as we were headed to church, I was skipping along ahead of him. Suddenly, my mother appeared and grabbed me. My father rushed over and tried to pull me away from my mother. There I was in mid air with Mother pulling me by the feet and Father pulling me the other way with his hands under my arms. I was kicking to get loose, and unbeknownst to me, I was hurting my mother, as I found out later.

I was not aware that John, Ray, and Dolly were parked nearby and observed the entire scene. Suddenly John appeared and grabbed Lester from behind and pulled his arm around his back, pushing upward until he gave up. We then hurried to the car. I jumped into the back seat with Ray and Dolly, and we sped away. I cannot begin to put into words the happiness I felt at that moment. I had just been kidnapped and I loved it.

My Uncle Joe, Aunt Gen, and my cousins Jimmy and Joey had moved to a community near Lake Worth, Florida, called Green Acres. And that's exactly where we were headed.

I want to stop here and advance forward to when, at the age of sixteen, I went to Chicago to work for a time and stayed with my father. While I was there, he showed me some letters that my mother had sent him after they had been divorced for a while. I read these letters many, many times, and each time I would get a lump in my throat. In the letters she apologized to my father for what she had done and asked him to forgive her. She explained that she never did really love him and she was just looking for a father for Dolly. He told me that he had forgiven her, but the letters were so sad that even though I read them many times, I could almost feel the pain that my mother felt as she poured out her heart in great detail. I respect her ever so much for doing that.

There was never any doubt in my mind that she really loved John Spetz, and he loved her. They seemed so happy together and it made for a good home environment.

So here we go, lickety-split, from Chicago, Illinois, to Lake Worth, Florida. What a fun trip that was! We were all together and happy as larks. It seems like we sang and laughed most of the way.

Uncle Joe and Aunt Gen welcomed us with open arms, and we were happy to see our cousins Jimmy and Joey again. Grandpa Gallo had moved in with Uncle Joe and Aunt Gen, and he was also there to welcome us.

I don't think any of us children had ever been out of Chicago, and Florida was like a dream. We ran around barefoot most of the time with just a pair of shorts and sometimes a T-shirt. It was such a great place! It was almost like we were on vacation. This was early in the fall of 1946, and there was more to come.

Ray, his wife Jean, and Bill

Aunt Gen, Bill, sister Dolly — mid 1990s

2 The Florida Experience

FLORIDA WAS SO MUCH FUN for Ray and I. Cousin Joey was our constant companion since he was closer to our age. Playing was the name of the game at this point in our lives as we explored the surrounding areas, played by the canal which was about a block from the house, and went fishing and swimming as often as possible.

Every morning we would hit the door as soon as we could, for another day of fun. Ray and I had been apart for what seemed like a long time, and we were on a mission to make up for lost time. This was definitely a fun time in our lives, after the turmoil of a divorce, a custody battle, and just being apart.

It was the fall of 1946, and Ray turned five on October 20th of that year. I was still four years old and had lived in the house on Massasoit, another house in Chicago, Grandma Payne's, and now Uncle Joe's — four different places in my short life. I had also been hit by a car and severely burned my left leg.

In Florida

23

The trauma of these events was lessened somewhat by the fact that I was so young that my memory was blurred on a lot of the details. Suffice it to say that a broken home was the root of all the problems that had developed so far in my lifetime. In this book, I am attempting to show the devastating effects upon children when they have to go through the trauma of a broken home.

It was not very long before we were made aware that a major hurricane was headed our way. It was the fall of 1946, and our family was busy getting ready for the hurricane by boarding up all of the windows and doors. I don't think "evacuate" was in anyone's vocabulary back then. It seemed like people just buckled down and rode it out.

This was one scary time. We were all in the same room, trying to stay calm as the wind and rain pounded the house. There were a lot of noises coming from outside as we could hear debris hitting the house. We could also hear branches breaking and feel the house shaking. Everybody was quiet. Fear has a way of causing people to be quiet. Even as a child, I could sense the fear that was dominating the room.

Believe me, there was not much talking. Everybody had a worried look about them. Ray and I huddled against Mother, simply because that seemed to be the safest place to be, as she held her arms around both of us. Mother was about five or six months pregnant at this time.

Then it happened. *Blam!* A loud noise came from the kitchen. It was loud — *really loud* — and it was scary — *really scary*. Grandpa Gallo had walked into the kitchen and he immediately started cussing in Italian. He could really rattle off the cuss words, although we did not know what most of them meant.

Uncle Joe and John walked into the kitchen to see what had happened. I don't think we knew the details until later, but a palm tree had fallen on the roof right over the kitchen area. Fortunately, it wasn't big enough to break into the house and nobody was hurt. We had roof damage, but I am not sure how severe it was. Even though nobody was hurt, I know the whole household was suffering from rattled-nerves syndrome.

I don't remember how long the storm lasted, but it seemed to end abruptly. The wind stopped blowing and it became very calm. It was over, and we were all thankful that we had survived.

We did not see much of Dolly during this time. She was in and out a lot, and I attribute that to the difference in our ages. She was now a fourteen-year-old. Since she was close to Jimmy's age, they often did things together. Ray and I were with Joey most of the time. He was a couple years older than us, and we learned a lot from him about outdoor things like critters, snakes, and alligators. There were alligators in the canal and they sure were scary looking to me, so we kept our distance. I don't remember them ever being a problem.

Soon Dolly had a boyfriend coming around. He was either in the military or had just gotten out, because he came to the house

Dolly in Florida

several times in uniform. His nickname was Salty, and that is what everybody called him. I never knew his real name. As I got older, I often wondered why Mother let them date, since Dolly was only fourteen, and Salty was obviously at least eighteen or older.

One day Dolly left with Salty and did not come home. Mother was frantic! I remember her calling everybody, including the police, who came to the house to talk with her. They finally located Dolly and Salty, only to discover that they had gotten married. Dolly thought she did not have to come home since they were married.

Not to be! Because of Dolly's age, Mother had the marriage annulled and Salty was forbidden to ever come to see Dolly again. We never saw or heard about Salty after the annulment. Dolly was very unhappy because Mother had her marriage annulled, and she probably became rebellious because of it.

Soon after this affair, Dolly was on her way to Chicago where all her friends were located. She stayed with Grandma Gallo and completed her high school education in Chicago. For the next three years or so, Dolly would come home to live with us only in the summer months and return to Chicago to go to school.

I had started calling John Spetz "Dad." For clarification in the rest of this story, I will refer to him as *Dad* and my birth father, Lester Payne, as *Father*.

After the hurricane in Florida was over, the men took the boards off the windows. Then they began opening the windows in order to get air flow through the house. One window was stuck, and Dad, using the palms of his hands, began forcing it upward to open it. His hand slipped and his arm went right through the window. What a sight! It immediately started bleeding profusely.

Mother and Uncle Joe took him to the hospital to get the wound stitched. It was a very nasty cut that extended from near his wrist to the bottom of his elbow. It left a scar that was visible for the rest of his life.

One day, when Ray and I were in the house, Mother approached us frantically and said, "Quick! Both of you — hide under the bed."

We wanted to know why, but she told us that she would tell us later, so we quickly crawled under the bed. Mother knelt down

Uncle Joe

to make sure we were well under the bed with nothing showing. She told us to remain completely silent and not to utter a word.

We couldn't imagine why we were doing this, but we knew by Mother's actions that this had to be very important. We could hear people talking and saw the feet of people walking by the bed. We were obviously totally puzzled. Finally, after what seemed like a very long time, Mother came into the room and said, "Okay. You can come out now."

We were told to get under the bed because my mother and Uncle Joe had spotted a police car pulling into the driveway and two officers getting out. They immediately knew what this was all about. My father, who had custody of me by court order, had somehow found out where we were staying and had the police looking for me. I had been kidnapped, and this was a felony charge waiting to happen.

The police informed them that they were looking for me and asked if I was there. Uncle Joe told them that I wasn't, and they asked if they could have a look around, to which he consented. This story might have turned out much differently if those officers had looked under the bed, but they didn't.

I think my mother and father reconciled after that because he never again tried to get custody of me by using legal means. The fact that he never exercised his legal custodial rights again actually hurt him in another custody battle that would follow about four or five years down the road. I think my father finally realized that I needed to be with my mother, and they started talking and being civil to each other.

Some years later, Ray and I spent a few summers with my father and his new wife, Marie. As my parents' relationship improved, my father and Marie came to Ironwood to visit us on one occasion. We all sat in the living room and talked. My dad was nowhere to be found. It was just my mother and father, Marie, and Ray and I. We had two sessions with them on two consecutive days, but I was never comfortable with it — not one bit! I was always afraid of my father because I thought his ulterior motive was to take me away from my mother. I could not wait for them to leave.

We settled down to a happy life. The weather was nice and we were not far from the beach. We would go there fairly often and my mother, who was very much pregnant by this time, would go with us and sit on a blanket and watch us, along with Dad. Ray and I loved the beach, and it was a new and wonderful experience for us. It was so much fun splashing and playing in the waves.

We would often all go together with Uncle Joe, Aunt Gen, and Jimmy and Joey, even including Grandpa Gallo at times. We would pack a picnic lunch and eat at a picnic table in the park. We would sit on the edge of the water and wait for a big wave to splash against us. We had never been around salt water before and that took a little getting used to. Yes! The beach was a wonderful place to be for a couple of young boys.

It was hard to have a relationship with Grandpa Gallo because of the language barrier. He had been in America for many years, but had lived mostly in Italian neighborhoods in Chicago. We could talk to him — he would understand a little of what we were saying, and then smile.

But he also had a temper. He loved to wear hats and most of them were white. I don't remember which one of us kids did this, but Grandpa Gallo had set his prized, white derby hat on a chair, and one of us sat on it and crushed it. Now it was time to run for the hills. Grandpa was really angry and went on a rampage as he tried to find out which one of us did it. We all disappeared because that seemed like the logical way to handle the situation.

My mother was very close to her father, as was Uncle Joe. They were both raised to speak Italian and had no problem communicating with him. Not so with Aunt Gen and my dad. Neither of them knew Italian.

Aunt Sadie was still living in Chicago close to where Grandma Gallo lived. She and her husband, Uncle Ivan, had two girls, our cousins Kathleen and Charmaine. They came down to visit a few times and would later move to Florida. Dolly, who lived with Grandma Gallo during the school year, also lived with Aunt Sadie part of the time.

Dad with Barbara

The day finally came when Mother went into labor. Uncle Joe and Dad took my mother to the hospital in Uncle Joe's car. However, there was a slight problem in that she didn't get to the hospital in time. My dad delivered my sister, Barbara Jean Spetz, in the back seat of Uncle Joe's car. Barbara was born on Thursday, February 6, 1947.

My mother was brought to the hospital for clean-up and a few day's stay. Ray and I had a baby sister. *How neat is that?* I thought she was the cutest thing ever. Mother would let us watch as she breast-fed her. Wow! Nobody ever had told me about this part. I remember touching her little hands and feet and wondering how in the world feet that little would ever be big enough to walk and how hands that tiny would ever be able to hold anything.

Mother with Barbara

Dad worked for a car mechanic in Green Acres, not far from where we lived. He had done mechanic work in the service and seemed very adept at it. However, I never felt he was happy in Lake Worth because most of his family, including his mother and father, lived in Ironwood, Michigan. I believe he longed to go back there. He had spent many of his younger years working in the woods in the Upper Peninsula of Michigan, and that was where he longed to be.

Dad came from a large Finnish family. There were a total of thirteen siblings counting him (one was stillborn), and most lived in the Ironwood area. Obviously, he had been talking to his younger brother Waiko about all of us moving to Ironwood since he did not want to continue living in Florida. I am sure that he felt out of place in Florida. He also knew if we continued to live there, we would eventually have to get our own place — I don't think he wanted to do that.

I guess he talked my mother into moving to Ironwood because she contacted Grandma Gallo in Chicago and arranged for a loan for us to be able to afford the move. Ray and I did not want to leave Florida, but Mom and Dad kept talking about how much snow they had up there and how we could play in the snow. And since we really did not have any choice in the matter, we accepted the fact that we would be moving, and perhaps it would be fun after all.

We had become close to our cousins, especially Joey, and that was probably the hardest part of moving. He had become like a brother to us. We would also miss Uncle Joe, Aunt Gen, and Grandpa Gallo.

Uncle Joe had come to Florida after the war ended and he was discharged from the military. He had been a Radio/Radar Instructor in the U.S. Air Force. After WWII, he became Lt. Col. Commander of Group V, Civil Air Patrol. In 1949 he founded the Gulfstream Realty & Insurance Agency, which later became Gallo Insurance & Realty in Lake Worth. He was a Lake Worth City Commissioner and Vice Mayor, and he also chartered the

Uncle Joe

Commerce National Bank. He was a charter member of the Lake Worth Exchange Club, and later he was the President of the Florida Exchange Club.

Years later, I picked up the book titled *Who's Who in Southern Florida*, and he was listed in it. He was a very successful businessman and well-respected in the community. He was an honest and very compassionate person, and family was at the top of his list of priorities. He was my role model and I loved him very much.

Surprisingly, he had a lot of Finnish clients. Later in life he told me he enjoyed them because they were straight-up people. When they told you something, you could count on it because they kept their word.

Also later in life, we had the opportunity to go on several trips together, and I was fortunate enough to attend his and Gen's fiftieth wedding anniversary and also a big extravaganza that he put on for Grandma Gallo's one-hundredth birthday in West Palm Beach, Florida.

Now it was time to move to Ironwood, so we loaded up our belongings and headed north. We would live with Uncle Waiko and Aunt Ruth in a farmhouse in Ironwood Township until we got on our feet and were able to move to town. My dad and Waiko would be working together in the woods.

Many adventures and a lot of fun were just around the corner and we were optimistic. I was on the way to my fifth residence at the age of five years.

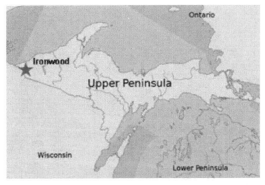

Ironwood is the westernmost city
in the Upper Peninsula

3
The UP (Upper Peninsula)

HERE WE ARE ON THE move again. We were headed to Ironwood, Michigan, which is located in the Upper Peninsula and is simply called the UP by most. To be specific, we would be living in Ironwood Township.

There is a common expression about the UP today that wasn't in use years ago. The people who live or have lived in the Upper Peninsula are called Yoopers. A lot of fun and jokes are connected with this title. It is considered an endearing term to those with ties to this peninsula.

The small city of Ironwood was a thriving, bustling place during this time period. Iron ore mining and logging were enjoying their heyday, and were the two staple industries for the western end of the UP, where Ironwood is located.

Logging in Ironwood-Bessemer area

In the fall of 1947, before school started, we arrived at Uncle Waiko and Aunt Ruth's house. This would be our first introduction to them, their family, and most of the rest of Dad's family who lived there. Dolly had been sent to Chicago to live with Grandma Gallo and

Aunt Sadie while she attended Lindbloom High School in Chicago. Mother went to Chicago several times during the school year to see Dolly and Grandma Gallo. She usually went alone by train, which was a cheaper way to travel at that time. Ray and I went with Mother the following year on one of her trips.

Ray and I did not arrive in Ironwood Township with a great deal of expectation. We left Florida and our cousins, Uncle Joe, Aunt Gen and Grandpa Gallo, and some neighborhood kids with whom we had become acquainted. We were moving to a completely different environment where we did not know anybody.

Uncle Waiko and Aunt Ruth's house

Uncle Waiko and Aunt Ruth had a daughter named Little Ruth. There is a bit of a strange twist here. We often hear of a son named after his father with the name Junior attached to him. In this case we have a daughter who was named after her mother. They were called Big Ruth and Little Ruth. We had no problem because we called them Aunt Ruth and Ruthie. Ruthie was our age and we had a lot of interaction with her. Ray and I took to her almost immediately. She was a live wire, full of energy, and easily excited. She was quick to smile and laugh, and seemed to enjoy everything we did. Even today, I smile when I think of her.

It wasn't long before Dad took us around to meet some of his other brothers and sisters who lived in Ironwood Township. We went first to visit his sister, Jenny, who was married to Alfred Ranta. What a shock and pleasant surprise we had when we first met them. They had a set of twins, Arthur and Wesley, who were paternal twins and our age. They also had a set thirteen months younger, Margaret and Marie, who were also paternal twins.

Think about this for a minute. Art and Wes were born on March 3, 1942, and Margaret and Marie were born on April 27, 1943. In a span of thirteen months, Alfred and Jenny went from zero children to four children. Imagine the workload for a mother under those circumstances. Wow! We were really racking up the cousins fast on the Spetz side of the family, and we loved it.

Twins seemed to run in the Spetz family. Uncle Waiko had a twin brother named Art, who we never did meet since he lived in another state. We did get to meet Tom and Sam Spetz, Dad's brothers and paternal twins, who lived in the area. Neither of them were married nor had any children. Tom did hook up with a woman named Stella a few years after we met him, and they finally married. Stella ran a bar in Hurley, Wisconsin, called the First and Last Chance. Hurley was a twin city to Ironwood and was separated by the Montreal River, which was really more like a creek than a river. Her tavern was the first place when you crossed the state line into Hurley.

We loved Tom and Stella. A few years later, after we had moved to town, they would come and visit, and Stella always had a sack of candy for Ray and me. Now if that doesn't make a kid love you, nothing will! Sam never did marry, and I have some pleasant memories of him even though I was not around him very much. He would buy us candy and get down on the floor and roughhouse with all of us kids.

Dad also had an older sister named Mary whom we met. She had married Richard Niemi and they had four girls and one boy. Three of the girls, Nelmi, Florence, and Ida, were much older than us and ended up being good friends with Dolly. Ray, their only son, was also older than us. But their other daughter, Susie, was a few years younger. Susie was Uncle Sam's pick-of-the-litter. He absolutely adored her.

So here we are, Ray and I, the new kids in town. Barbara was only about seven months old at this time and not walking. We loved our little sister, but she was too young to go outside with us, which is where we practically lived.

Ironwood Township was a unique place and so different than any other place we had lived. I am sure it was a big adjustment for Mother also. She had been born and raised in Chicago and

Sister Barbara

always had good living conditions, including indoor plumbing and a bathtub. Now, for the first time, we would be living in a house that did not have indoor plumbing. There was an outhouse sitting there waiting for us to get used to, and a sauna for bathing.

Living in the same house as Uncle Waiko and Aunt Ruth was no big deal. We had a lot of family living around us at the house on Massasoit, and we were just coming from living with Uncle Joe and Aunt Gen. This was common back in that day. Families were more apt to include other members besides their immediate family. This was a big aid in helping people get on their feet financially.

Waiko's house was close to the airport in the township. This was a small airport, but it was an airport nonetheless. To give you an idea of how small it was, the terminal was one room, the size of a storage shed. There was some air traffic back then, but not much.

Most transportation at that time was by train. It was the glory days of passenger trains. Ray and I ended up making the trip from Ironwood to Chicago and back, via the Chicago and Northwestern railroad, many times during our childhood.

Mother and Father had reconciled to the point that she was sending us to Chicago to spend a couple of weeks with my father and Marie in the summer of 1949 and 1950. Mother would put Ray and me on the train and ask the conductor to watch over us because we were by ourselves. We probably went back and forth from Ironwood to Chicago five or six times, but the most fun was when we traveled alone.

Train station in Ironwood

The conductor kept an eye on us, but he allowed us to roam from car to car when we were moving. We would go in the dining car to eat, and the conductor would pay for our meal. I think Mother must have given him the money. It didn't seem like it took very long for everyone on the train to realize we were by ourselves, and they went out of their way to be nice to us.

On the trains, we especially loved the grandmotherly ladies, who would ask us to come and sit by them. Ray and I would always oblige because they were very generous. Some of them gave us candy and some gave us money. It was a great feeling because they made us feel special.

Some of the fondest memories of my childhood were when Ray and I took those train rides together. My father was always at the station in Chicago to pick us up. And when it came time for school to start in the fall, he would put us back on the train that would take us home to Ironwood. These were the best trips of all.

We both loved our mother very much and we missed her terribly during the two summers we spent with my father, and she probably missed us just as much. She would come to the train station in Ironwood to pick us up and burst out crying as soon as she saw us. This was followed by a lot of hugging.

Mother would always have special treats prepared for us when we got home. She was a wonderful baker, and she would have cookies, cake, or pies waiting for us. She also would outdo herself at meal time. She was a great Italian cook, and she knew Ray and I loved spaghetti, ravioli, and homemade bread with olive oil and parmesan cheese on it. That was some of the food we were raised on — and we loved it. It was food that we didn't get when we stayed with my father.

I have some guilt feelings when it comes to my father. I never did love him like perhaps I should have. Ray and I both looked at John Spetz as our dad. My father was always fair with us, and his wife, Marie, was super nice to us. We were treated well when we stayed with them for the summer.

But it was not the same as being with Mother and Dad. I held it against my father because he took me away (legally) from my mother in the custody hearing in Chicago. I never trusted him after that because I thought it was his intention to do that again. He was also a very strict disciplinarian, which is not all bad, but a lot of love has to be mixed in with all of that discipline or it is not very effective in the grand scheme of raising children. It can easily be interpreted as being mean.

Mother was just the opposite. She was probably too easy on us, and I am sure she spoiled us. I really believe that God, in His wisdom, ordained the fact that children should have both a mother and father in order to balance each other. If one is missing, it is easy for a child's life to be out of balance.

Dad, Mother,
Barbara, Ray, Billy

Dad's parents, who were both retired, lived in a small house not far down the road. Meeting them was a unique experience. They were older Finnish-speaking people and could not communicate in English. Grandma Spetz would smile a lot when we tried to talk to her in English, but people could not understand her for the most part. Grandpa would spend most of his time talking to Dad, who could speak Finnish fluently. Mother would just sit there and smile, without talking.

Grandma knew that kids liked candy, but they never had any. She would motion to us to come near and hand both of us a Vicks cough drop. Neither of us liked Vicks cough drops, but we did not want to hurt Grandma's feelings as she would be displaying a big smile as she handed one to each of us. Ray and I did the same thing with the cough drop — we would put it in our mouth and park it on one side until we left, then spit it out. We visited them many times and ended up spitting out a lot of Vicks cough drops. I did love her for doing what she thought would make us happy.

John Spetz and
Uncle Waiko

Uncle Waiko and Dad would do things for them to help them out, and so would a lot of the family. Because of their large family, there were a lot of visitors. Later, the family would move the house onto Aunt Mary's property. In that way, Aunt Mary could be close by to help them as they became older.

We quickly became very close to all of our UP family. Of course, we were around Ruthie the most because we lived with them, but we spent a lot of time at the Ranta's playing with Art and Wes, and Margaret and Marie. Ray and I would spend the night at their house on many occasions.

We would visit Aunt Mary and Uncle Richard Niemi quite often also. On many Saturday nights, we would go there to have a sauna. This was in and of itself a very unique experience for Ray and I. Dad went with us most of the time and showed us exactly how to go about taking a bath.

Ironwood Township was comprised of a very high Finnish population. I am not sure why they settled there, but I have heard it said that the weather was comparable to the weather in Finland, and so they felt at home. Most Finnish families built a detached

Stove and hot
water tank

sauna and that was how you got extremely clean without taking a tub bath. There were not many bathtubs in the township back then.

An old-fashioned outside sauna is an interesting concept. You have a building with two rooms. When you enter, you are in a long narrow room that is called the changing room. This is the room where you take off all of your clothes before entering the main sauna area, which is the steam room.

Once inside the main sauna area, there is a wood-burning stove with a cradle of rocks on top of it. A round tank attached to the stove is filled with water that heats up as the stove gets to burning well. There is another tank, away from the stove, filled with cold water. Most saunas did not have running water, and the water had to be carried into the sauna, perhaps from a hand pump on an outside well near the sauna. However, most of them now have running water. When people fired up their sauna, it was deemed ready for use when the water was hot.

There were three long benches that reminded me of a chicken coop. They were like stair steps, and it was hotter the higher you sat. Wash buckets and dippers were available inside the steam room.

On entering the steam room, you would take a wash bucket and fill it full of water, using hot and cold water to get

Steam room

the temperature of the water to your liking. Finally, you took a dipper for water and sat on the top bench. You then threw water on the rocks from time to time to create more heat from the steam.

Sometimes you were able to sit and endure the fast rise of the temperature until you started perspiring profusely. If you got it too hot, you would come down to the second bench or even to the lowest bench and wait until it became bearable, and then go back to a higher bench. If it was still too hot, you could step out into the changing room since it was always a lot cooler.

After you had perspired enough, you would come down and sit on the bottom bench and soap up from head to toe, rinse yourself, and finish by dumping a pail of water over your head. We had to be careful about not using too much water if there were other people to follow us in taking a sauna.

Coming out of the sauna, you felt like a new person and much cleaner than you would taking a conventional shower or bath. As we got older, we would team up and go to the sauna together. It was like a social event.

My favorite sauna buddy was Art Ranta. We went together many times, solved all the world problems, and figured out who were the prettiest girls in school. All this while taking a sauna.

One Saturday night when Art and I went to the sauna together, it was really cold outside. It was well below zero degrees and there had been a huge snowstorm the day before. We were probably thirteen or fourteen years old at the time. We sat on the top bench talking, and Art was explaining a little about the Finnish culture in relationship to taking a sauna.

Naturally I took him at his word on everything he said since he came from a Finnish family and had always lived in the UP. He explained that in Finland you were not considered a man unless you left the top bench while perspiring, ran through the changing room, and dove into a snowbank. This intrigued me since I had heard of people diving into icy water in the winter time. What a challenge that must have been!

So I asked him if he thought we should do it. His reply was an emphatic, "Absolutely! You want to be a man, don't you?" I agreed and he said, "You go first — I'm not sweaty enough. I will go when you come back." So I went straight out the door and dove into a large snowbank.

I thought I was going to die. It was below zero outside and I wondered if it was possible to die from such a shock to a person's body. I scrambled back to the sauna as fast as I could, wanting to quickly get back on the top bench. Guess what? Art had locked the door on me. Here I was standing outside the sauna, butt naked, in the below zero temperature, pounding on the door. Fortunately, Art did not want to be responsible for my death, so he quickly opened the door.

Now! Get this! He thought it was funny and was laughing his head off. I scrambled back into the sauna to warm up and he was still laughing.

In a few minutes I said, "Okay, buddy, it's your turn."

I will never forget his reply: "Do you think I'm crazy? You would probably lock the door on me."

And so it was. We both laughed and told this story many times to our friends. I loved Art like a brother and we had many good times growing up together.

Now it was time to start school, so Mother enrolled us in Roosevelt School in the Township, very close to where we lived. She enrolled us under the names of Bill Spetz and Ray Spetz. We thought that was our name now, since Mother had married John Spetz. Our kindergarten teacher was Mrs. Olson, and she was a very loving person with an excellent reputation. She would remain in that position for many years to come and her list of former students grew every year.

We were so happy to have cousins Arthur, Wesley, and Ruthie in the same class with us. They helped us feel at home since we did not know any of the other kids. Kindergarten was fun to me. We got to draw, color, and look at pictures in books. I never did like it when we had to take a nap every day. I couldn't understand why I had to take a nap when I wasn't tired or sleepy. Go figure! I loved recess time. That made more sense than taking a nap. We got to go outside and play until the weather got cold and it started to snow. Then we would play in the gymnasium.

Roosevelt School in Ironwood Township

Children back then did not know half as much as children do now. Television wasn't available yet. Consequently, no one had a TV. In later years, with the emergence of children's shows like Barney and The Muppets, children would learn a lot before they even entered school. All we ever did was play and color in coloring books. Today's children have a big edge on those of us who started school back in 1947. Many of today's children are computer savvy by the time they start school.

One thing that I remember in kindergarten brings this point home. One of the first things we were taught in kindergarten was to count to one hundred. I really struggled with this for some reason. I could count to ten when I started school and I thought that was great. Now they wanted us to count to one hundred.

You've got to be kidding me! I would get mixed up and have to start over. To this day, I do not know why that was so hard, but one thing I remember for sure was that I was the last one in my kindergarten class to learn to count to a hundred. Mrs. Olson had everyone stand up and clap when I finally did it. I can't remember if that made me feel good or bad. Hmmm!

When our kindergarten year was over, I had turned six years old and had lived in five different places. Just around the corner we would be moving again and we would be living in the sixth place in six years, so the average of having a different residence every year of my life would still be intact.

I mention this fact because it seems that this constant moving around contributes toward instability in a child's life. It is hard on a child to continually be uprooted from a school or neighborhood where they have made friends, and be taken to a completely new environment where they do not know anyone. In our case, we would not have been moving to all of these places if our home had not been broken.

Unless we come to grips with the reality that broken homes are at the root of much of the cycle of violence and poverty that is so vividly displayed in this country, no proposed solutions will be forthcoming.

So here we go again. All of us would be moving from Ironwood Township to the town of Ironwood. Living with Uncle Waiko and Aunt Ruth had become comfortable for us as children. We were being uprooted from Roosevelt School and our friends. We would be going to a new school, not knowing a soul.

4
The Curry Street Years: Part 1

THE TIME FRAME FOR THE Curry Street years was from the spring of 1948, after we finished kindergarten at Roosevelt School and moved to Ironwood, until moving to the woods in Wakefield, in the winter of 1950. We rented a house at 106 N. Curry St., which was just a few short blocks from the Central Grade School where we would be attending first grade under the tutelage of Mrs. Smith, a very nice teacher.

Our second grade teacher was Mrs. Talaska, who was equally as nice as Mrs. Smith. Mrs. Talaska seemed to be there to help any of us who needed it, and always with a smile. After we finished second grade at Central, Mrs. Talaska was moved up to teach third grade. We were pleasantly surprised when we started third grade that she would be our teacher again, although we would only have her until late November when we moved to the woods in Wakefield.

Central School

There was a church on the corner of Ayer and Curry Streets. Our house was the first one on Curry after the church, but today that house is no longer there. We could look straight across the street and see St. Ambrose School, which faced Ayer Street. Our yard was kind of small, but we did have a front yard and a back yard to play in.

The greatest improvement was the fact that we had — are you ready for this? — *drum roll, please!* We had indoor plumbing for the first time in about a year, which included a bathroom with a bathtub. We were uptown now. How about that?!

We loved our house. It had three bedrooms. Ray and I had a bedroom, and Dolly, who was there for the summer, had her own room and shared it with Barbara, who was in a crib at that time. We were so happy to welcome Dolly back again, and she seemed to love being home with us and our mother.

We were fortunate to be able to spend the summer getting to know the kids in the neighborhood, and again, playing outside was the name of the game. It was nice to be able to get acquainted with some of the kids before school started.

It was great to have Dolly back for the summer. She would take us places that were within walking distance of our house, which included downtown Ironwood. She was the one who introduced us to the movies.

We would all walk downtown and attend the Ironwood Theatre and sometimes the Rex Theatre. This was absolutely one of the most exciting things we did. You have to remember that there were no television sets in those days, and we were immediately enthralled with the Western movies. This was the cowboy era, and we were all into that. Roy Rogers,

Ironwood Theatre

Gene Autry, Lash LaRue, and Hopalong Cassidy were among our favorites. All of these cowboys were bigger than life to us.

Then there were the very funny sidekicks, like Gabby Hayes with Roy Rogers, and Smiley Burnette with Gene Autry. We loved them, too. There were expressions used back then that you don't hear in this day and age. One of these was "Stick 'em up!" This came from the cowboy movies of the day. It was what the person holding a gun would say to the person they were pointing their gun at. It simply meant for them to hold both hands over their head. This was a very serious command. If the person didn't comply or reached for their gun instead, they would be shot.

Mother, who always bought Ray and I the same thing on each of our birthdays, had bought us belts and holsters that contained two six shooters. It's what Roy Rogers had, and she knew that was what we wanted. They were so neat and looked like real guns, even though they were cap guns. Cap guns were great, great, great! They not only looked like real guns, they sounded like them, too.

A lot of the neighborhood kids were getting cap guns also, and we had fun playing Cowboys and Indians. The kids who didn't have guns had to be the Indians. None of us real cowboys would even think of being an Indian. We had been brainwashed by the movie industry into thinking that the Indians were savages who burned down the settler's houses and went on the warpath, and that they were all enemies of the cowboys.

The kids who were the Indians went and hid. It was our job to find them and shoot them. (Believe me — I know what is going through your mind.) So, when we found them, we would shoot and they were to play dead until we found and shot them all.

I loved my mother, but she made a big mistake by buying us both BB guns, a rifle that shoots tiny metallic pellets. Attention to all mothers out there: *Do not buy BB guns for your young children. Do not let them talk you into buying them a BB gun.* When they say, "Other kids in the neighborhood have BB guns, why can't we have one?" Or when they promise not to aim the BB gun at anyone and promise not to shoot at anything they aren't supposed to shoot at, don't give in to them.

We loved it when she presented them to us for one of our birthdays. These were much more like real guns, compared to cap guns. These were rifles, and all the cowboys in the movies carried rifles in their scabbards. They shot real bullets. Well, not really, but close enough — they shot tiny copper balls.

Mother tried to get us started right, but the problem was she couldn't watch us all the time. First, she bought us some targets that we set up in the back yard where it was safe. This worked for several days but soon became very boring. I don't know to this day why shooting out windows with BB guns was so much fun back then, but it was. I don't know if it was the tinkle of the glass breaking or the feeling that you are in charge of this demolition project. Maybe that was it. Maybe it was an ego thing. It could have been the feeling that you had a gun in your hands and you were capable of doing damage with it.

There was a vacant house in the neighborhood, and it so happened that one day there were about four of us "on patrol" in our neighborhood. We all had BB guns and we were looking for action. I don't know who came up with the lame-brained assumption that the house was haunted, but we all started believing this to be the case. We walked around it several times and tried the doors and windows, only to find they were locked. We really wanted to explore inside the house to see if there were ghosts living in there.

Finally, we managed to open a basement window. Now we had a major problem. Who was going in first? One of the kids finally volunteered if we all promised to be right behind him. The window was not at ground level, so we helped to lower him into the cellar. After we lowered the second kid in, I was going to help Ray into the cellar. Then I was going to stand guard outside — brave me.

Before I could lower Ray in, we heard one of the kids scream. They both came out with their eyes looking like they were going to pop out of their heads. It scared the hell out of us. We started to run away when another of the kids started hollering for us to help him out of the window. We didn't want to hang around to do that, but we overcame our fear, even though we were scared to death.

Now we were all outside and there did seem to be safety in numbers. Plus, we all had our guns. We asked what happened and why the first kid had screamed.

"I saw a ghost in there," he said.

A ghost? That was it. The war was on. It was an all-out assault. We opened fire on the house, breaking most of the windows. It seemed like the logical thing to do. We were doing the owner of the house a favor by breaking the windows so the ghosts could get out. It made sense to us.

We did get into trouble for this at a later date, but not before we had a chance to do some other things with our BB guns to amplify our problems. Shortly thereafter, maybe a day or two later, I had been to Bob's, the little store down the street, and I had my BB gun with me. Across the street, near St. Ambrose School, one of the neighborhood kids was walking on the sidewalk minding his own business. I have forgotten his name so let's call him George. Bear in mind that I was on one side of Ayer Street and he was on the other side.

I raised my BB gun and aimed at him and said, "Stick 'em up, George."

He looked at me and said, "No!"

I was thinking, *What is wrong with this kid? Doesn't he know he is supposed to stick 'em up?* I couldn't back down, so I told him, "If you don't stick 'em up, I'm going to shoot you."

He was sure I wouldn't, so he said, "No!" again.

I was young and I knew better than to shoot him with my BB gun, but I was going to make it look like I did. Just before I pulled the trigger, I lowered the barrel of the rifle down toward the road. Oh, wow! I still can't believe it. The BB bounced off the road and hit George right in the forehead.

He screamed, "You shot me!" and put his hand over his head and lit out for home crying.

I was really scared now. I knew I was in big trouble. There would be no excuse I could come up with to justify this. George's mother came to our house shortly after that, and Mother made me go into another room while she talked to her. I was probably shaking by now. Fortunately, George was all right, and at least I had that going for me.

Here is where Mother was a little crafty. A police officer used to help us kids cross the road on our way to school, and Mother would walk with us to that point and would often engage in conversation with him. She had gotten to know him fairly well.

Mother told me that since what I had done was so bad, she had to call the police. Anyway, she called the police and arranged a little meeting between the police and me. A policeman came over to the house in uniform to talk to me, and I was really nervous. He explained that because of what I had done, I could go to Reform School, an institution where youthful offenders are sent as an alternative to prison. But since George wasn't hurt very badly, he said that he would do what he could to help me out.

I guess if it was possible for a little kid to have a heart attack, I would have had one. I also remember him telling me that if I ever shot anyone again, he wouldn't be able to help me, and I would go to Reform School for sure.

Then it was my mother's turn. Her main emphasis was that I could have very easily hit George in the eye and he could have been blinded because of me. She took my and Ray's BB guns away from us for a very long time. At this point, she did not know about the incident with the house where we shot out the windows.

I was a big baseball fan as a child — I mean really, really big. I listened to all the Detroit Tigers baseball games on the radio. My mother couldn't get over the fact that I would lie on the floor and listen to every game from start to finish, unless interrupted for some reason. I had a huge collection of baseball cards (I wish I had them today!) and would get them out and go through them, arranging them by teams and positions.

I was up on all the baseball statistics. I knew the batting averages, home runs, and RBIs of all the players on the Tigers team. I would pour over the Ironwood *Daily Globe* newspaper's sports section and always knew who was leading the league in every category. Ray didn't share my intense interest in baseball, although he liked to play ball with the neighborhood kids, as I did.

One day, I had come into the house and taken out my baseball cards to play with them. Ray had walked across the street to where some kids were playing softball in the front yard of St. Ambrose School. I was in the living room playing with my cards, and I heard my mother call to me from the basement, where she was washing clothes. She wanted me to come downstairs and talk to her.

I wasn't sure what she wanted, but I bounded down the steps. She had her purse on a table next to where she was wringing out clothes on what would be, in today's world, an antique washing machine. She reached into her purse, took out a piece of paper and some money, and handed them to me. She said, "I want you to go to the store for me and pick up a couple of things. Here is a list and here is the money."

Ray and I had made this trip many times, and it was always for just a few things. Mother did the major shopping at the A&P grocery store in downtown Ironwood. But when we ran out of an item or when Mother had forgotten to buy something during her weekly shopping, we would go to Bob's store, just down the street from where we lived.

I liked this because Mother would give us a nickel to spend when we were there. That doesn't sound like much, but most stores had a penny candy counter with a glass top so you could look down into it and pick out what you wanted. Some of the candy was two for a penny, but most were one penny. We would get five pieces of candy, and there was usually a little drama involved because it is really hard to divide five pieces of candy between two brothers. Since Ray was across the street playing ball, I could go myself and keep all the candy. That sounded good at the time.

I will never forget this. I got to the top of the stairs on the way to the store, and my mother called me back. "Come here, Billy. I need to tell you something." She had a grave look on her face when she spoke. She said, "I had a dream last night that you came to the door screaming and blood was running down your face. I want you to be extra careful today." I could tell by the look on her face that she was troubled, and it caused me a little concern at the time. I quickly dismissed it, though, and was on my way.

I had to pass St. Ambrose School on my way to the store, and I saw Ray getting ready to bat. I decided that I wanted him to go with me because we always did this together, so I asked him. He didn't really want to go. He wanted to continue playing ball. Then I tried to bribe him and it worked. I said "If you go with me, we will split the candy and you can have the extra piece."

He replied, "Okay, but let me finish batting."

Ray was always stronger than most kids his age and he had a big roundhouse swing. On the first pitch, he swung and missed. I was standing a little closer to him than I should have. His bat came around and hit me above my right eye, directly on my eyebrow.

I remember falling to my knees and feeling dazed. I could feel the blood running down my face and I swiped at it with my hand. When I saw blood all over my hand, I panicked and started running for home, screaming for Mama. She opened the door just about the time I got there, and the very first words out of her mouth were, "I knew it."

She grabbed me and put a towel over the wound and told me to press really hard. She got some gauze and tape and fixed it to the point where it was not pouring blood. Ray was right there also.

Since we didn't have a car, we walked to downtown Ironwood. She took me to the doctor's office, which I remember being on the second floor of one of the buildings. I guess in today's world he would have stitched it up, but instead he used metal clamps. So, I had five metal clamps on my eyebrow which would later have to be removed — very painfully, I might add.

In later years, I talked to my grandmother, aunt, and uncle about my mother, and they all said the same thing. Grandmother was the most vocal, saying she thought Mother had a gift because she would have visions that she called dreams, and they would come true. She related at least three stories of this happening when Mother was still living at home. My aunt and uncle told me some stories also that were kind of haunting. Of course, I told them of this incident and they weren't surprised a bit.

One day I got the bright idea to get my ball and bat, toss the ball up, and hit it with my bat onto the sloped roof of the church next to our house, but not over the church. Then I would catch the ball when it rolled off. This was great fun, and I did it long enough that I was getting pretty good at it.

About this time, Mother appeared at the door and shouted, "You better quit that right now! You are going to break a window." All the church windows were stained-glass, and now I understand her concern, but not then.

I was having fun, and she was going to make me quit. She reiterated what she had said, telling me to quit and come in the house. She turned and walked back inside. *Hmmm! I'll just do one more — she probably won't see me since she went into the house.* Yep! The ball went right through one of the stained-glass windows.

Mother must have heard the noise because she came out right away. She scolded me and took me into the house and sat me down. I thought I was probably going to get a spanking, but she had a different idea. The parsonage for the church was right around the corner facing Ayer Street. Mother told me to go over to the pastor's house and tell him what I did. She also said to tell him to get the window fixed and give us the bill, and we would pay it. She also informed me that I would have to work off the debt after she paid for the repairs.

Okay, so here I go to talk to the pastor. I was really nervous. When he came to the door, I told him that I broke the window and then burst out crying. I don't remember if I was crying because I was really sorry for what I had done, or because I wanted him to have mercy on me. He bent over and put his hand on my shoulder and told me that everything would be all right and that he would talk to my mother about it. Later. Mother told me that the pastor called her and said that since I came over and apologized, they would take care of replacing the window.

So, I got out of that one too. Thinking back, I wonder how much that stained-glass window cost. It was a large window. I just wished I would have listened to my mother. I never did realize what I put Mother through until I had children of my own. Parents are special people — the only problem is that as children, we don't realize that.

Even though we now had our own bathroom and bathtub, we would always go to either the Ranta's, Waiko's, or Niemi's every Saturday night to take a sauna. Dad loved going to the sauna and Mother did also.

We usually went into the sauna two at a time. When we were at the Ranta's, Ray would usually go with Wesley and I would go with Art, but sometimes we changed that around. When we went to Uncle Waiko's or the Niemi's house, Ray and I would always go together. For the most part, children did not go with their parents if they were old enough to know how to wash themselves. I have fond memories of going to the sauna and wish I now had one in my back yard.

We were allowed to spend the night with Art and Wes and Margaret and Marie on quite a few occasions, and that was always our hope when we went there. Sometimes Art and Wes would go home with us and spend the night, but we did spend more nights at their house than they did at ours. We no longer went to the same school, and we really treasured these weekend encounters. It was always fun to see Ruthie also. We had become very close after going to kindergarten together.

I think it was somewhere around November of 1948 that we found out Mother was pregnant again. We were excited that we would be having a new brother or sister. During this time, you did not know until the baby was born whether it was a boy or girl. Mother would have her hands full with Ray and me, and Barbara, who was one year and ten months old at this time. I remember Mother calling Dolly in Chicago to tell her about her pregnancy. Dolly was at Grandma Gallo's for the school year, and I remember Mother and Dolly discussing her pregnancy and laughing about it.

We finished first grade and were now off for the summer of 1949. I was seven years old and had caught up with Ray, at least for the time being. Dolly had come home to spend the summer. Not long after that, Mother gave birth to my brother John William Spetz on June 30, 1949. This was so cool. We had a baby sister and a baby brother. Mother would let us watch while she fed the baby, and we both thought that was so neat.

I remember wondering how in the world the baby didn't choke to death because it seemed like he would not stop long enough to breathe. We would giggle when Mother would burp the baby. Later we would go to her and say, "Make the baby burp again!"

Our family was getting larger. Mother had her hands full with four children at home. She really appreciated Dolly helping around the house after Johnny was born. Dolly would not only help Mother with the chores, she loved to take care of baby Johnny.

Washing clothes was a big job when we lived on Curry Street. We had an old wringer-type washer in the basement. I don't think there were clothes dryers back then. Be that

Brother Johnny

as it may, we sure didn't have one. Mother would wash the clothes in the basement, wring them out, put them in a basket, carry them up the stairs to the back yard, and hang them outside to dry on the clothesline. There were no Pampers back then, so she washed all the diapers, and also hung them outside. Ray and I would help a little, but not much. We would bring her clothes pins when we were within earshot and she called for us to do so. I know she didn't have us do much because we stayed outside playing all day.

5 The Curry Street Years: Part 2

WHEN WE LEFT FLORIDA TO move to Ironwood Township, Grandpa Gallo was still living with Uncle Joe and Aunt Gen. Shortly afterward, he moved to California where he had some close friends. While he was there, he was struck by a car and injured. Uncle Joe went to California to pick up Grandpa Gallo and bring him to our house on Curry Street so Mother could take care of him.

I am not sure how badly Grandpa Gallo was hurt in the accident in California, but soon he seemed to be fine and was getting around very well. I remember him sitting in the back yard repairing shoes at a little table. He seemed to be very adept at that; perhaps he was a shoemaker at some point in his life.

Grandpa Gallo

Grandpa Gallo discovered that there were a lot of Italians living in Hurley, Wisconsin, which was within walking distance of our house. After a simple walk through downtown Ironwood and down the hill, you would cross the Montreal River bridge — the state line — and be in Hurley. After Grandpa Gallo established these new friendships, we didn't see much of him on weekends.

51

Grandpa was a meticulous dresser, and people in general dressed up when they went to town, especially to any kind of event. Hurley was quite the party town, containing, rumor has it, somewhere in the neighborhood of a hundred taverns with most of them on Silver Street, which runs right through the center of the downtown area.

Silver Street, Hurley, Wisconsin, in 1949 — daytime and nighttime

Ironwood and Hurley were bustling with business at this time, with logging and iron ore mining going wide open. A lot of gangsters used to frequent Hurley, including Al Capone. It was probably like a vacation for him to come to a small and friendly Italian town, miles away from his crime empire in Chicago. The population of Ironwood, Hurley, and the entire western end of the Upper Peninsula diminished greatly when the iron ore mines closed because of the increased expense in mining and processing the ore. Logging also slowed down to a snail's pace as most of the virgin timber was logged out.

Every Friday, for some time, Grandpa Gallo would dress up in a suit and tie and head to Hurley for a weekend of drinking and fun. We would not see him again until Sunday afternoon. Grandpa Gallo was funny. He could not speak English very well and could not say Hurley. He would call it "Curly."

Later that year, Grandpa Gallo became very sick and was confined to a bed, while Mother took care of him. She made the dining room into a bedroom for him so that he could be on the first floor.

One day I was upstairs when I heard my mother scream. It was the most terrifying scream I have ever heard and I was frightened. I immediately ran down the stairs to where my mother was standing near Grandpa Gallo's bed. She was now crying profusely. I had no idea what was going on.

"What's wrong Mama?" I asked, as I approached her. She stopped me before I got to the bed where Grandpa Gallo was lying. She was sobbing as she ushered me out of the room. I still did not understand what was going on, and I was frightened. I asked her again, "Mama, what's wrong? What's going on?"

She finally answered me between sobs, saying, "Your Grandpa passed away."

I was stunned. I knew people died but it never dawned on me that someone in my family would die. I thought, *How could this be? He is my Grandpa; how could he die? Now I won't have a Grandpa anymore.* I was seven years old and I began to cry along with Mother.

Ray was outside playing and came in the house just about the time I started crying. He saw Mother and me crying, and he began to cry also, even though he did not know why we were crying. I finally told him that Grandpa Gallo had passed away. He immediately started crying even louder. Mother came over to us, knelt down, and put her arms around us as she gathered her composure.

These were some sad times at our house. Uncle Joe came to Ironwood and took Grandpa Gallo's body by train back to Chicago to be buried. Grandma Gallo had bought cemetery lots for her and Grandpa years before, and she wanted him to be brought back there to be buried. Mother went to Chicago for the funeral, but she did not feel like it was a good idea for us to go with her. I shall never forget Grandpa Gallo.

Mother with
Grandpa Gallo

Soon after we moved to Curry Street, Mother started taking us to church on Saturday. She had been raised as a Seventh Day Adventist, and we always went to church when we were living with my father in Chicago. She had stopped going to church about the time she and my dad started their affair. We never went to church the entire time we were in Florida or when we lived in Ironwood Township. I think Mother had a change of heart because it was about this time that she wrote letters to my father apologizing for doing him wrong.

There was a small Seventh Day Adventist church in Ironwood on Florence Street. It was in a residential area and looked like a white house. Years later, after I had left Ironwood, the congregation moved to the church that was next door to us on Curry Street. This was the same church where I broke the stained-glass window.

Mother quickly made friends and became very close to Irma Barron, who lived in the Township. She and her husband Archie had four children: Dennis, Glenda, Albert, and Ethel. We visited them many times while we lived on Curry Street, and they came to visit us almost as frequently.

We all became very good friends, except for my dad. I don't think he wanted my mother to be an Adventist, and his actions toward her friends bore this out. When he came home from work and they were at our house, he would barely acknowledge them. Then he would disappear.

Be that as it may, it did not deter Mother from continuing her relationship with them. Irma Barron and Mother became very close. Glenda, who was two years older than Ray and me, babysat all of us quite often. She was kind and loving, and I was fortunate to see her over the years. Dennis was like a big brother and Ethel was like a younger sister. Albert was more our age, and we played with him a lot.

We never saw Dad much during the week because he was busy working in the woods, logging with Uncle Waiko and other loggers in the area. We would spend time with him on weekends when we would go to Little Girls Point on the shore of Lake Superior and to Black River Harbor, which flowed into Lake Superior.

We would go swimming at Sunday Lake in Wakefield, and I thought that was the cat's meow for swimming. The water was calm, and much warmer than Lake Superior. It quickly became our favorite place to swim. We did things on weekends including picnics and going shopping with Mother. Saturday night remained a staple in our life because that was sauna night.

Billy and Ray

Second grade at Central School went along pretty smoothly, and I became good friends with a kid in the neighborhood named Jim Hoskins. We were in the same grade and both loved basketball. I was able to put the ball in the hoop a higher percentage of the time and could feel myself improving. We spent hours playing behind his house where he had a basketball hoop attached to his garage. Jim was a starting center for the Ironwood Red Devils during the late 1950s and into 1960.

54

It had been very traumatic for Ray and me when Mother first approached us, early in the summer of 1949, about going to Chicago to spend a couple of weeks with my father. I thought this might be a ploy by my father to keep us and not send us back.

No! No! No! We didn't want to go to Chicago. We both started crying, begging, and pleading with Mother to please not make us go. Dolly was home for the summer, Barbara was a little over two years old, and the baby (Johnny) was to be born on June 30th.

She finally got us to quit crying and settle down. She then tried to explain that he was our father by birth and that he really deserved to see us.

We didn't care about any of the logic, but here again we were doomed. We had to go.

So, my mother took us to the train station in Ironwood and put us on a train to Chicago where my father would pick us up at the Northwestern train depot in Chicago. He would then take us to where they lived in Broadview, a suburb of Chicago.

After we all tearfully said good-bye at the train station, the train ride turned out to be a lot of fun. Here we go again. We were only seven years old, and this would be the seventh place in which we had lived.

I cannot say enough about the trauma that children go through simply because of a broken home. I realize that there are situations where a divorce is inevitable, but there are just as many divorces that could be avoided if parents would make a heartfelt effort to go for counseling and do whatever it takes to work things out. Everyone knows that it is hard on children when their home is torn apart, but I don't think everyone realizes just how hard it really is. It can be totally devastating, and if children do not receive support of some kind, it can lead to a life consumed by total unhappiness.

It is very hard on a child to be taken out of a school and neighborhood where they have friends, and then taken to a new school and a new neighborhood where they do not know anyone. When this is done, often a child begins to feel a sense of not belonging anywhere. This is one of the steps that can lead to an inferiority complex.

Children need to have stability in their lives to feel secure and happy. They need a loving father and mother, friends, and family. I realize in a lot of cases this is not possible, but it is a goal that we, as parents, need to strive for if we want our children to be normal and healthy.

Since about fifty percent of marriages end in divorce, is it any wonder that our society as a whole has suffered? If you are married with children and are contemplating a divorce, please, please reconsider. Exhaust every avenue available to reconcile before doing so. I am not asking for myself, I am asking for the children who usually do not have a voice in the matter. I am asking for the very small children, the middle-age children, and yes, the teenage children.

My whole purpose of writing this book is to give people a perspective, from the eyes of a child, on just how hard it is on them when their family is falling apart. You will see in the following chapters how a broken home affected me for many years. Most of the drama that I went through is yet to come.

6 Lost in the Snow

RAY AND I HAD RETURNED to Ironwood from spending the summer with my father in Broadview, and we were still living on Curry Street. We were in third grade at Central School with Mrs. Talaska as our teacher again. It was October 20, 1950, and Ray had just turned nine years old. I wouldn't be nine until May 9, 1951. Life was great and it was a happy time in my life.

My dad was a partner in the logging business with Uncle Waiko. They had just completed a logging assignment in north Ironwood Township and were getting ready to do a huge job east of Wakefield, Michigan. They would be jobbing from Paul Steiger, who was considered Mr. Logger in this part of the country. He was a super nice guy, well-respected, and seemed to have his hands in everything that had to do with logging, at least in the western end of the Upper Peninsula.

Ray and I were excited on this day as my dad and mother announced to us that we would be moving to the job site to live. Yes, we would be living in the

Loggers

57

woods. A bunkhouse and cook shack were being constructed on the site and we would be living in the cook shack. My mother would be doing the cooking, and she seemed to be excited, too.

My brother and I had mixed emotions about leaving our friends at Central and transferring to a school in Wakefield, where we didn't know anybody. However, the excitement of living in the woods offset our anxieties to a great degree. I'm not sure exactly how long it was after that before we actually moved, but I think it was Thanksgiving weekend because we were there several days before we had to go to school.

Uncle Waiko's logging camp

It was just as much fun as we had imagined. My mother not only did the cooking, but she also kept the books and did the payroll. Looking back, she really had her hands full because there were four of us kids. Besides Ray and me, there was my sister Barbara, who was three years old, and my brother Johnny, who was only a year and a half.

Imagine that workload. She had to wash clothes by hand and hang them all over the cook shack. She did have an iron, but it was the type that had to be heated on the wood stove because we had no electricity. We liked it when she ironed, because that was when she would tell us stories.

Mother did have a helper who was referred to as the "bull cook." His main job was to help with whatever she needed. This included fetching water in buckets from the spring just down the hill from the cook shack, and splitting and carrying in wood for the wood cook stove and potbellied wood heater. He also had responsibilities pertaining to the bunkhouse. The lumberjacks would stay in the bunkhouse until it was time to eat. Then they would come to the cook shack where we had a very long table and benches for them to sit on.

Ray and I were in our glory. We helped the bull cook with his job during the day when we got tired of playing and exploring. We especially liked going up to the bunkhouse to visit the lumberjacks when they finished work for the day. They would give us candy and make us promise not to tell our mother, just in case she didn't want us to have any. They told us stories (there were no radios or TVs in the woods!) that would capture our undivided attention. I still remember some of them to this day, especially the funny stories.

Now the dreaded part came into play. We were to start school in Wakefield. We sure didn't want to go, but we realized that we had no choice in the matter. My dad drove us from the camp on a logging road that had been bulldozed. I'm not sure how far it was from the cook shack to US 2, the main road, but I do know it seemed like a very long way. Dad stayed with us until the bus came and picked us up. I remember him asking the bus driver what time he would be dropping us off after school. Then he promised the driver that he would be there to pick us up. It had begun to snow that morning, but it was not very heavy and no one seemed to be concerned.

I guess school went as well as could be expected, but we were sure glad when it was over so we could go back to the woods. The snow that was falling lightly in the morning was turning into a blizzard with swirling winds, and the snow began to drift across the road. The bus driver was driving slower than he did in the morning, and we realized he was having visibility problems.

We finally reached the spot where Dad would pick us up, but there was no one there. The bus driver told us not to worry because our father would be there shortly. To this day, I can't believe he just dropped us off in a blinding snowstorm and left. Now we were looking at the logging road that was quickly getting drifted over and wondering what to do. That was when Ray said, "This is not the right road. This is not where we got on this morning."

I was shocked. There were no cars on the road and it was snowing so hard we could barely see. I remember asking him, "If this is not the right road (he was always more observant than I was), then where is the right road?"

"I think it is farther down," he said.

So we went trudging down the highway in a blinding snowstorm to find the right logging road. We were on US 2, which was the main highway going east from Wakefield.

There were no businesses or houses in sight, and all the cars seemed to have disappeared. We were walking into a blizzard with the snow stinging our eyes. I was very much afraid because there seemed to be no solution to our problem. I know Ray was also afraid, but we did not confide in each other on this point. We refrained from crying even though that seemed like the logical thing to do. I think we were both trying to stay strong for each other. I don't know how far we walked, but I remember thinking, *What if we never find the right road?*

Finally, after what seemed like an eternity, Ray exclaimed. "Here it is. This is the right road."

I looked at it and couldn't tell much difference. It was drifted over like the last one, and there still was not a soul around. I trusted Ray's instinct, and we decided to start walking toward the camp.

Anyone who has ever lived in the UP knows that you don't dress as warm for school as you would if you were going to be outside for a long time. We began to get cold — as in *real cold!* Walking was difficult because the snow was getting deeper and deeper, and eight- and nine-year-old kids do not have very long legs. At first, we tried to cheer each other up by saying it probably wasn't that much further. We couldn't figure out why no one was there to meet us.

It was beginning to get dark, but we could still see the outline of the road as we started down a hill. There was a little creek at the bottom that we had to cross. This gave us a little confidence that we were on the right road because we remembered the little creek. Then we started thinking that the other logging road we had been on probably had the same creek crossing it.

We were scared, tired, and very cold. Walking was becoming more and more difficult, and we stopped to rest. This didn't work very well because it seemed colder when we stopped. We didn't rest long before we started trudging again. Finally, we were so totally exhausted and cold that we decided to stop and lay down with one of us lying on top of the other one to try and keep warm. Ray laid on top of me first, and it did help some. I was a little bit warmer. Then we would switch, and I would lay on top of him for a while. All the while we were getting totally covered with snow.

It was during this time that we started becoming convinced that we were going to die. We started talking about heaven and wondering if there really was such a place. We sure hoped so because we wanted to see our mother, dad, sisters, and brother again. We knew we were beginning to freeze to death.

Then something strange happened to both of us. We were no longer cold! I found out later that the body starts to shut down when you begin the process of freezing to death.

Then it happened! I felt something kick me in the ribs and I heard someone cry out. It was my dad! He was on foot looking for us, and since we were covered in snow, he didn't see us and ended up tripping over us and falling down.

My dad had twin brothers who were also working for him and Uncle Waiko. Uncle Tom, one of the twins, was the bulldozer operator and his twin brother, Uncle Sam, was a mechanic. What had happened was that my father couldn't get out with the car, so Tom was going to bulldoze the logging road ahead of him. The only problem was that they could not get the dozer started. The three of them were feverishly working on it when my dad decided to leave them there at the camp and go on foot to find us. All the while he was hoping that the bus driver had decided to just take us back to the school.

Dad

So here we were. He found us! This was probably one of the happiest moments in our lives. He got us up and hugged us as he shed a few tears.

That was when I discovered that I couldn't walk. My feet felt like lead weight, and I couldn't move them. Ray (he was always tougher than me) seemed to be okay and could walk just fine. So now my dad had to carry me on his shoulders. I know that it was hard on him to walk in the deep snow and carry me. We stopped to rest fairly often.

Then we heard this beautiful sound of the dozer. Tom and Sam had gotten it running, and it was coming our way. We stepped to the side of the road as Tom approached on the dozer with a big spotlight showing the way, since he was dozing the road at night.

He stopped and talked to us, and Dad told him to continue on because they had logging trucks coming in the morning. That was when my dad told us that if he hadn't come ahead, Tom would never have seen us and would have run over us with the bulldozer. I thought about it later and realized if my dad had been walking on the other side of the logging road, he would have walked right past us. Now Dad could walk quicker because we were on a cleared road. I wished I could walk, because I knew this was hard on him.

When we got to camp, my mother swung the door open before we even got to it. She burst into tears as she checked us out. Since Ray seemed to be all right, she set me on a chair and poured warm water in a pan and had me soak my feet. It turned out that my feet

Snow around a cabin

were severely frostbitten, along with my ears. Fortunately, my hands were okay. To this day my feet do not perspire, and I do not have much feeling in them. Ray was fine. I never have figured out why. Maybe he just had better blood flow or something. Anyway, go figure!

That was the last day we took the school bus. During the rest of the school year we were taken to school and picked up. I believe our lives were spared that night for a reason, and I am thankful to God because I really believe He intervened. I know my mother was praying, for sure.

After we got past this mind-boggling incident, things seemed to level off some, and we returned to life in the woods. Ray and I continued to go to the bunkhouse and spend time with the lumberjacks. They seemed to really enjoy us coming to see them. I know we had fun with them. A lot of them played poker every night before going to bed, but the ones that didn't were the ones we spent the most time with.

Payday was on Friday and most of the loggers were ready to head to Hurley for the weekend. They had been working hard in the woods all week and were ready for a weekend of drinking and socializing with other lumberjacks from the area.

Typical logging scene

Ray and I would often go with Dad on Sundays to hunt for the ones who had drank too much and were stranded in Hurley. We knew them all by name and would help Dad find them as we went from tavern to tavern looking for them. Some of them were passed out, and Dad would literally drag them out of the tavern and put them in the car because he needed them to work the next day.

Oftentimes we would make several trips to round them all up. Sometimes when we got back to the camp and let them out, they would fall in the snow. Then we would have to help them get to their bunk so they could sober up and hopefully work the next day.

We were now moving into the early spring of 1951 and Mother informed us that she was pregnant. Again, we were very happy to know that we were going to have another brother or sister. Mother continued on with her heavy workload while Dad was making plans for us to move to the town of Wakefield by early summer. He realized that she would not be able to keep up her heavy workload in her latter months of pregnancy. I do not know who took over for her when she left, but I know Dad wanted to live in Wakefield so he would not have to travel as far to get to work.

During our time living in the woods, we had stopped going to church, simply because of Mother's workload and the fact that it was quite a distance to Ironwood. Archie and Irma Barron would come out to the woods to visit us at times. We would look forward to their visits because we had kids to play with.

We moved to Pierce Street in Wakefield just about the time school ended in June. Living in the woods was the eighth place that Ray and I had lived, and when we moved to Wakefield that would be our ninth residence. Our average of one residence a year was back on track.

Typical Upper Peninsula blizzard

7 Moving to Pierce Street

HERE WE GO AGAIN. MOTHER and Dad had rented an apartment on the second floor of a house on Pierce Street in Wakefield, Michigan. We had enjoyed the time in the woods, but for the first time that I can remember, we were ready for this move. There were no neighborhood children to play with in the woods, and we knew there would be companionship if we moved to town.

It was early summer, and Mother was definitely showing signs of her pregnancy. We were all happy to be in a house with indoor plumbing, a bathroom with a tub, and running water. Wait! Let's not forget the electricity. Here we were uptown again, and loving it.

It did not take Ray and me long to find some playmates. The Anderson family lived a few doors from us on the opposite side of the street. They had three boys, two slightly older than us and one our age. The one we knew the best was Hans Anderson. I was quite impressed to see that Mrs. Anderson had written a book titled *I Married A Logger*. I had never known anyone who had written a book, and I thought that was so neat.

There wasn't a playground close by, so we played in the street. I don't remember anyone objecting to our using the street as our playground. We played softball and football in the street with many of the other neighborhood kids joining us. When a car came along, which wasn't too often, they would drive slowly and then stop to give us time to get out of the way. We really didn't like these interruptions, however few, but we did not have any choice.

Since we were living in Wakefield, we were close to Sunday Lake where we went swimming fairly often. Mother would come with us and sit on a blanket, like she did when Johnny was a baby.

There were rides to Ironwood Township for sauna on Saturday nights. As soon as we got settled in, Mother started taking us to church in Ironwood on Saturday for Sabbath School and church. We were happy to be around the Barron kids again. Irma and Mother had become close friends, and Glenda would come to babysit while Irma and Mother went shopping.

I thoroughly enjoyed Glenda. She was kind to us and had a big smile that seemed to be contagious. We would go to their house sometimes after church to eat lunch. Dad came by to pick us up in the late afternoon to go take a sauna. He was just in and out and never did stay very long.

Dolly had gotten married in Chicago while we were living in the woods. Ray and I had gone to Chicago to visit Dolly when we lived on Curry Street, and we met her boyfriend, Frank Page. She ended up marrying Frank, but none of us were able to attend the wedding. Now that Mother had a telephone, she spent a lot of time talking to Dolly, who was eighteen years old at this time.

Frank and Dolly moved to Wakefield so Dolly could help Mother during the last few months of her pregnancy. Dad had consented to have Frank work for him in the woods when they got here. Frank was a big, strong guy who was six feet, two inches, and weighed over two hundred pounds. He sure fit the mold of a lumberjack quite well, and he always made me think of Paul Bunyan.

Everyone was excited when they arrived. This was great! Our whole family would be living together again, with the addition of our new brother-in-law Frank, and another addition expected to arrive in just a few months. Although Mother was getting fairly big by now, she seemed to stay pretty busy and her health seemed fine.

Our menu at home greatly improved from when we were at the logging camp. At the camp, Mother had to cook for a lot of people, so we ate mostly stew, potatoes, chili, and things that were easier to make in large quantities. Now Mother started showing her expertise as a great Italian cook, and we had Italian food along with some of her other specialties. She was very adept at making bread, cakes, pies, and many other desserts.

Do I think that nobody could cook as well as my mother? I absolutely do, but then, I am sure thousands of people believe the same about their mother. I was raised on her cooking, and I was a little biased. She went back to making homemade bread. After taking it out of the oven, she would cut it while it was still hot and give anyone who was around a slice of warm bread with olive oil and parmesan cheese on it. Yum! Yum!

Finally, the day came. Ray and I were again playing in the street when Dolly came and told us that Mother was in labor and they had to take her to the hospital. We immediately went running home, expecting that we would be going with Mother to the hospital and staying until the baby was born. Mother hugged us and explained that it would be better for us to stay at home, and that Irma would be coming over in a few minutes to take care of us while she was gone. We were told it would probably be for three days. We were disappointed but accepted the fact that we couldn't go.

Dad and Mother left immediately, while Frank and Dolly waited for Irma to arrive. When Irma arrived a short time later, Frank and Dolly took off to the hospital to be with Dad and Mother.

It was sometime in the afternoon on September 14, 1951, and here we were. Ray and I were nine years old. Barbara was four and a half, and Johnny was a little over two years old. This was going to be so nice. Soon we would have a baby brother or sister. and there would be five of us kids living at home, plus Frank and Dolly. Irma was smiling and seemed excited as well.

Ray and I asked Irma if we could play outside since there was nothing much we could do. She consented and told us that she would cook supper and call us when it was ready. We never seemed to sit still when we were children. We loved the outside — inside was very boring to us. Remember, there were no cell phones or TVs. We did get a radio eventually, but we didn't have one at this time. Most of the time when we were called in to eat, we went reluctantly because we always seemed to be in the middle of a game.

Irma called us in to eat supper, and our first inquiry was, "Has the baby been born yet?"

She replied, "Not yet, but probably very soon." After supper, Irma read us a story, said a prayer with us, and tucked us in bed.

We hoped that when we woke up in the morning, there would be good news about our new brother or sister.

The next morning when Ray and I got up, Irma was in the kitchen cooking us a nice breakfast. Our first question to her was, "Has the baby been born yet?"

She replied, "Yes," and that it was a boy. We were so happy and wanted to know the name of the baby. She said that she didn't know because everyone was still at the hospital. We decided that we might as well go back outside until someone came home.

We were playing football in the street with our neighborhood friends when we noticed that Frank and Dolly had come home. We went bounding up the steps to see them and find out what was going on. Irma was in the kitchen and we scurried past her into the living room where Frank and Dolly were sitting on the couch.

"Where are Dad and Mama and the baby?" we inquired.

Dolly looked tired and she didn't appear to be in a good mood as she answered, "They are still at the hospital."

"When will they be home?" we asked.

"I don't know for sure. When a woman has a baby, they usually have to stay in the hospital for three days." She spoke slowly and softly, and we figured it was because she had been up all night.

The waiting game was still going on. We concluded that there was nothing we could do, so we went back outside to play. We noticed when we passed Irma that she didn't seem to be in a very good mood either. We figured that was all right because everyone would be happy again when Mama came home with the baby. We were really looking forward to seeing our mother and new brother.

We went back to playing football and did not even have a clue that something was wrong. We never noticed that Dad had come home, but we looked toward the house and there he was, walking our way. He looked so different. We were used to seeing him in his logging clothes, and now he was in a white short-sleeved shirt and slacks. We ran to meet him, all excited, thinking Mother and the baby were home and this whole ordeal was over with.

The first words out of our mouths were, "Where's Mama and the baby?"

His head was bowed down and he didn't answer. I remember thinking, *What's wrong with him?*

Then he raised his head and looked at us with swollen, red eyes and said, "Your mother is dead!"

No! No! No!! This can't be.

We both broke down. He put his arms around us and we all cried alongside the street. I don't know how long we were there, but we finally walked toward the house. By this time, I was so weak that I could hardly make it up the steps. We were both crying out of control and wondering what had happened.

When we got inside, Irma started crying and hugging us also. We went to the living room where Frank and Dolly were sitting. Frank was just staring at the floor and Dolly was sitting next to him with swollen eyes and a blank look on her face.

We had questions. "What happened?" "What about the baby?"

Dolly looked at us as tears rolled down her cheeks. She never answered — it was like she couldn't talk.

Irma, sensing the situation, came into the living room and put her arms around us again and said, "Your mother passed away, but the baby is fine."

We found out later that when my mother was giving birth to my brother Ronnie, she began to hemorrhage. She was in a small hospital in Ironwood, and they couldn't give her blood because they didn't have her blood type. They sent someone to the larger hospital in Ironwood (I think it was the Grand View Hospital) to obtain the needed blood. When they got back with the blood, it was too late. She had literally hemorrhaged to death.

I loved my mother with a passion, and I know she loved me. I felt like I had lost the whole world. I know my stepfather cared for me, but it just wasn't the same. I suddenly felt like I had lost the only person who really and truly loved me. I felt alone all the time after that, even when I was with people.

Even though I am now in the latter stages of my life, I can unequivocally say that this tragedy affected me far more than any of the other traumas that I have endured throughout my entire life to this point. The memory of the days surrounding my mother's passing are etched permanently in my brain. They probably will be there until the day comes that my brain no longer functions.

I am not sure how Mrs. Anderson found out about Mother, but it wasn't very long before she came over, by herself, to see us. I was numb at this point, and not interested in anyone hugging me and telling me how sorry they were. I knew there was nothing anyone could do, and I had cried myself completely out of tears.

I did like Mrs. Anderson and was polite when she hugged Ray and me, and then Barbara and Johnny, but there were no more tears to fall at this time. She turned her attention to my dad, Dolly, and Frank and began talking to them.

Mrs. Anderson and her husband owned a cottage by a lake not far away. She asked to take Ray and me to the cottage for a few days and bring us back for the funeral. She felt that Dolly was going to have her hands full with Barbara, Johnny, and our new brother, Ronald Charles Spetz. She thought it would do Ray and me good to get away from the situation for a few days, and we both went along with the idea..

They had a boat hitched to a nice boat dock and all of us boys were allowed to take the boat out fishing or just ride around. The oldest Anderson boy did all the steering. Ray especially liked riding in the boat and always wanted to ride in the front and watch the bow of the boat part the water. That was fine with me; I liked the middle because it seemed more stable. It was very hard to focus on what we were doing, but we were trying the best we knew how. We fished for a while and caught a couple of small perch. We threw them back, since we knew we weren't going to eat them.

Going to bed was the worst part. All the thoughts about my mother came rushing through my mind, and I would start crying again. I did not want anyone to hear me cry, so I would bury my head in the pillow and finally drop off to sleep.

The next morning we got up for breakfast, but I could not eat. Mrs. Anderson encouraged me to eat, but I just couldn't. I wasn't hungry because I had a lump in my throat from the night before. My heart was heavy, and I'm sure it was evident in the way I was moving around.

After breakfast, swimming was on the agenda. I went through the motions, and so did Ray. Nothing seemed to be fun now.

SPETZ—Mary Spetz, nee Gallo, at Wakefield, Mich., beloved wife of John, fond mother of Rosemary, Raymond, William, Barbara, and John, daughter of Rose and the late Vincent, sister of Joseph Gallo and Sadie Knapp. Services Wednesday, 11 a. m., at chapel, 3424 W. 63d street. Interment Oak Hill. GRovehill 6-0090.

Mary Gallo Spetz obituary
Chicago Tribune — September 18, 1951

8

The Funeral and Aftermath

AFTER SPENDING SEVERAL DAYS WITH the Andersons at their cottage by the lake, the day came when we were to attend our mother's funeral. Mrs. Anderson decided to take Ray and me directly to the funeral home instead of dropping us off at our house. I am sure she talked to our family about this. That morning, she got up early and drove to Wakefield to get some dress clothes for Ray and me to wear. When we awoke that morning, she had all our clothes laid out for us. What a kind and thoughtful lady she was.

I don't know how far it was from their cottage to the funeral parlor close to downtown Ironwood, but it seemed like the drive took forever. My mind was racing again — I was really dreading this. The thought of seeing my mother in a casket was more than I thought I could bear. I had determined before we even went inside that I was not going to look into the casket. I did not want to see my mother dead. I talked to Ray and told him my feelings. He agreed that he didn't want to look at her in the casket either.

When we walked into the funeral parlor, one glance determined that the casket was in the middle of the room to our right. We immediately took a turn to the left and went to the back of the room. Chairs had been set up for the funeral, and we went and stood at the back of the room behind the chairs, with Mrs. Anderson at our side. I am not sure who was staying with Barbara, Johnny, and Ronnie. but they were not there. Dad, Frank, and Dolly came back to where we were and wanted us to go up to the casket and see our mother. We both refused. Dolly tried to gently take my hand and offered to lead me up to the casket. I pulled back — there was no way I could do it.

When it came time for the funeral to start, Dad wanted us to come up front and sit with the family and friends. Again, we refused, because sitting up front meant we could see Mother's face. Mrs. Anderson agreed to stay in the back with us during the ceremony. We appreciated her understanding and compassion.

Bill, Grandma Gallo, cousin Kathleen

After the funeral was over, Mother's body was placed on a train bound for Chicago. Grandma Gallo had made arrangements for Mother to be buried near Grandpa Gallo's grave. She had also arranged for another funeral service in Chicago which would be attended by her family and friends.

Dad accompanied Mother's body on the train ride from Ironwood to Chicago and stayed for the second funeral service before returning to Ironwood. None of the rest of our family went to Chicago. We all returned to our house on Pierce Street, with our sister Dolly now being our caregiver.

It was the middle of September 1951 when my mother passed away. Ray and I were not yet enrolled in a school in Wakefield, even though school had been in session since the day after Labor Day. We moved from Pierce Street in Wakefield to a much larger house on Ridge Street in Ironwood just a very short time after the funeral. I believe that Dad and Mother had rented this house before the baby was born. Our move to Ridge Street would be our tenth residence. Ray would be turning ten the first month we were in the house, and I was nine years old.

This was the nicest home we had lived in since we moved to the UP, but that was a small consolation after losing our mother. It was larger, but because of her absence it was a lonelier house. Dolly had enrolled us in Sleight School, which was within easy walking distance from our house. I imagine that entered into the decision to rent this particular house.

We had just settled into our new house and were still reeling from the loss of our mother when another traumatic event loomed over our heads. Since our mother had passed away, my father decided he would sue for custody of Ray and me, thus ripping us away from the rest of our family. In his earlier custody battle with my mother back in Chicago, he had won custody of me, and Mother had won custody of Dolly and Ray. After my mother kidnapped me and we all went to Florida, he made one attempt to find us by sending the police to look for us.

However, he and Mother reconciled and he agreed to let her keep me if he could see us once in a while. He never again exercised his custodial right to lay claim on me. He was Ray's official father, since he had adopted him as an infant. Now that Mother, who had legal custody of Ray, was gone, it seemed to him that he should get Ray back, along with me. I was afraid and very nervous. I knew that he was my natural-born father and that he had been awarded legal custody of me.

I was young but I knew that he had a good chance of pulling this off. This created renewed resentment for my father, a resentment that I had been struggling to overcome the past several years.

Dolly was opposed to my father gaining custody of us and vowed to do whatever she could to help in this upcoming legal battle. She constantly consoled Ray and me, telling us not to worry because it wasn't going to happen. Dad had employed attorney Charles Santini to represent him. My father had come to Ironwood and employed Larsen, a local attorney, to represent him.

My dad had previously used Charles Santini regarding legal documents, and Mother had really liked him. He was an Italian, and she was also. That in itself was the foundation for a good friendship. He would come to the logging camp in Wakefield when we lived there, in regard to Dad and Uncle Waiko's logging business.

When Mother knew he was coming, she would prepare an Italian dinner that he really enjoyed. He made a point to be at Mother's funeral, which endeared him to me from that point forward.

He came to our house shortly before the trial to talk to us. He gave me reason for hope when he told Ray and me, "You boys don't have anything to worry about. Just let Uncle Charlie take care of it. There is no way he is going to win."

The trial was held at the courthouse in Bessemer, Michigan. Ray and I were not allowed to sit through the trial portion of the pro-

Gogebic County Courthouse

ceedings. My dad, Dolly, Frank, and my father all testified. Irma was there to show her support, and I believe she also testified, along with some other friends.

Ray and I did not appear on the stand because of our age. The judge interviewed us in his chambers, one at a time. Both attorneys were present, and a lady who documented the discussions.

I went first, and as soon as the judge started asking me questions, I burst out crying. I said that I wanted to stay with my family, and that I did not want to go and live with my father. Then it was Ray's turn. When he came out, I could tell that he had been crying also. I asked him what he had said. He basically said the same thing that I did.

We had moved into the house on Ridge Street in the beginning of October 1951, and the trial was taking place in December. When the trial was over, the judge postponed his decision until after the Christmas holidays, which was pure agony for us. For us not to know whether or not we would be torn from our family, did not make for a very Merry Christmas.

Finally, the judge rendered his decision by saying he thought it would be cruel to take Ray and me away from our family and give us to my father. He also mentioned the fact that five years had gone by since my father had won custody of me, and he had never exercised his custodial rights during that period.

Thank you, Charles Santini! You are a great guy. I cannot put into words how happy we were. There were a lot of hugs going around when we received this happy news.

Now that the trial was over and the decision rendered, we could all be together, and we were happy about that. Through all this, my brother Ray was my constant companion. We were pretty much inseparable. We had been through a lot together and we were always there for each other. Now that the case was settled in our favor, we would be able to play with our friends without this big cloud hanging over us. And it felt good.

We had started fourth grade at Sleight School and were making new friends. Our teacher, Mrs. Young, was a small, gray-haired lady

with a heart of gold. I always thought she knew of our circumstances because she seemed to go out of her way to be nice to us.

I would like to mention two people
who unknowingly helped us through this
difficult time simply by being our friends,
schoolmates, and playmates. Thank you,
Don Aspinwall and Joe Kasieta.

Sleight School

Our happiness was short-lived, however, because Frank and Dolly decided to
move back to Chicago and leave us. It is so very difficult to portray
in words how hard this was on me emotionally. It had only been
about four months since my mother had died, and I was still crying
myself to sleep almost every night.

One of the problems with losing your mother at a young age is
that a child takes their mother for granted. They never remember
her not being there, and they certainly have never given any
thought to the fact that she may not be there in the future. The
bond had been building and solidifying since the child was born.

When children are young, parents — especially mothers —
stand in the place of God to them, and losing a parent is like eter-
nal separation. We have to keep this in mind when we are dealing
with children who are under the age of accountability and without a
mother. The mother is the adhesive that keeps the family together.
The entire family revolves around her, and when she is gone, families have a tendency to drift apart, as will become evident.

Things were happening fast. First, we lost our mother, then we
went through a very emotional custody battle, and now Frank and
Dolly were moving, all within about four months. When I became
a little older, I did understand and never held it against Dolly for
leaving us. I understood that she was married and didn't really have
a choice in the matter. But I wasn't older yet, and I couldn't believe
that she would leave us all, especially the baby.

There was the fact that Frank and Dad had a problem over
money. I have heard some of the details, but I don't think it would
add anything to this story, so I will leave it alone. Suffice it to say
that they were not getting along, and Frank and Dolly were leaving.

So here we are in the living room saying good-bye. I was crying,
Ray was crying, and even Barbara was crying. Johnny and Ronnie
were too young to know what was going on. When Dolly knelt
down to hug me, I didn't want to turn her loose. "Why can't you

take us all with you?" I sobbed. That was really an immature question, but then again, I was immature. It made sense to me at the time. She was crying also. I never thought for one minute that this wasn't hard on her, too. We followed Frank and Dolly out to the car and watched them drive off. I felt alone and afraid.

After Frank and Dolly left and Dad had placed Ronnie with Mrs. Jones (let's just call her that), he hired a lady to take care of us. Her name was Betty Honquist and she asked us to call her Aunt Betty. That seemed a little odd at first, but later it seemed normal. Betty was an older woman whose husband had died. She was by herself, so she took the full-time job of caring for us. She lived with us and stayed night and day except for the weekends.

This worked out well. Dad would work every day through the week and come home, and Aunt Betty would have supper ready for us. She was wonderful, and I really believe she cared deeply for us.

My sister Barbara started having issues about the time Aunt Betty came to stay with us. She had what we called convulsions. She would fall to the floor and have seizures to the point that she would start banging her head on the floor.

I was really frightened the first time she did this for fear she would really hurt herself badly. I felt so sorry for her because I was sure that all the trauma she was having in her life had a lot to do with the seizures.

Sister Barbara
1990s

Anyway, when Barbara would go into one of these seizures, Aunt Betty would swing into action. She would get on the floor with Barb and hold her to keep her from banging her head on the floor. It was difficult for Aunt Betty to do this because Barbara was squirming, kicking, and screaming, all at the same time.

Johnny seemed normal and was a very quiet child and not a problem at all. Aunt Betty would talk to me like I was an adult and tell me her feelings and thoughts on things. It seemed so nice to have a mother figure in the house again.

Ray and I went through fourth grade at Sleight School without much incident. We had begun to make friends and played with the neighborhood kids. Two other kids that I remember very well were Tom Bednar and Bill Grose. These kids meant a lot to us the whole time we lived on Ridge Street. They never knew what was going on in our lives, but we, for sure, needed them. Thanks, guys.

I asked Aunt Betty why we couldn't get Ronnie back, because she could take care of him. We wanted our brother back. He was living across the street, but we were not allowed to see him. This was a major hurt in my life at this time. Aunt Betty explained that Dad owed Mrs. Jones a lot of money, and Dad was not allowed to go over and visit Ronnie, and we were forbidden also. She explained that Dad had seen attorney Charles Santini about getting Ronnie back, but she didn't know where that stood.

It was the summer between our fourth and fifth grades. Ray and I were ten years old. Later that summer, before we started fifth grade, Aunt Betty sat me down to talk to me. I was pretty sure I knew what was coming and I was right. She explained that Dad had not paid her for quite a while and that she had to have money to live, so she had taken a job at the Greyhound Bus Station in downtown Ironwood. The station had a little café, and she would be working there as a waitress.

Oh no! She was leaving. I broke down immediately and begged her not to leave. She began to cry as she hugged me. She assured me that she loved me, but she had to do this, even though she didn't want to. Ray and I did go to see her several times when she was working at the bus station. One time when we went, she had bought both of us a new pair of pants and a shirt. She said it was a birthday present for Ray's birthday, which was October 20, 1952. He would be turning eleven.

Ray and I managed to take care of Barbara and Johnny for the rest of the summer while Dad worked in the woods. We had a deal worked out that I would take care of them in the morning, and Ray was free to go out and play or do whatever he wanted. I would then fix lunch for all of us, and he would take over. I then could go out and do the same.

Brother Johnny
1990s

We got through the summer of 1952 all right, but now that we were starting the fifth grade with Mrs. Kilpatrick as our teacher, it became a major problem. Dad was working every day, but he didn't seem to earn enough money to make ends meet. We continued our pattern of taking care of Barbara and

Johnny, even though school had started. This meant that we would both have to miss school for one-half of every day.

I started out the school year staying home in the morning while Ray went to school. He would return at lunch, and then I would go in the afternoon. We would do this one week at a time. Then we would change the following week, and he would stay home in the morning. Whoever was at home in the morning would fix lunch for all of us. Most of the time it consisted of tomato soup, and sometimes that was it. Other times we had some bread and lunch meat.

For supper, Dad would usually bring something home from the store to cook. Our job was to put potatoes on the stove and boil them before he got home. Mashed potatoes were an everyday food at our evening meal.

One day Ray and I decided to walk across the street and see if Mrs. Jones would let us see Ronnie. We were both nervous because we knew she was going to be hostile. She had let it be known that she did not want us to come over and try to see Ronnie. I would have never attempted this alone, but Ray agreed to go with me. We felt compelled to do this.

So here we go. It was wintertime and there was a set of steps going up to the landing of the back door There was no back porch. The steps were covered with snow, but we managed to climb them and knock on the door.

No one came to the door at first. Ray told me that I didn't knock loud enough. He said, "Let me do it." He knocked on the door so loud, I thought the house was going to fall down.

I said, "Why did you knock so loud? They are going to be mad if they ever come to the door."

He just brushed me off and said, "Maybe they are deaf."

Finally, Mrs. Jones came to the door with a scowl on her face and stared at us saying, "What do you want?"

"We just wanted to know if we could see our brother," I said.

I will never forget her response. She said, "Absolutely not! Don't ever come back again." Then she slammed the door shut.

We were heartbroken! I never did tell my dad about this incident for fear that he might not have liked us going over to Mrs. Jones' home.

We finished the first semester of fifth grade at Sleight School, and we both flunked. We never went back to Sleight for the second semester because we would be moving again.

9 Chicago Bound

AFTER FINISHING THE FIRST SEMESTER of fifth grade, we were in dire straits. We had lost our mother, our sister had left, and Aunt Betty had left about four or five months back. It was a lonely Christmas that year for sure. My dad had done his best to provide for us. After Mother passed away, all he did was work and come home. He didn't drink, and I never knew of him having a relationship with another woman.

Dad was devastated when Mother died, and I knew it was as hard on him as it was on us — perhaps even harder, if that's possible. The only time he would leave the house would be to go to the store, get a haircut, or run errands, but he always told us where he was going and approximately what time he would be back.

Years later, I found out from Dolly that as Mother lay dying, she had asked Dad to keep the family together. He promised that he would. One can only imagine how he felt at this point.

Since we moved to Ironwood, I never knew of him doing anything but working in the woods. I don't know if work was slow or if he wasn't able to work on account of the weather. All I knew was that we had no money and very little food in the house. There were a few nights when all we had to eat were potatoes. We would boil them in water, mash them, and eat them without any butter or milk, just potatoes.

It was at this point that Dad felt he had to take drastic action. He had contacted Grandma Gallo and asked her for a loan. She agreed and sent him some money. After consulting with Grandma, Uncle Joe, Aunt Sadie, and Dolly, they reached a decision. Dad would go to Chicago, stay with Dolly, and get a job, with the intention of saving enough money to come back to Ironwood, pay Mrs. Jones, and get Ronnie back. Ray and I were dropped off at Grandma's in Chicago to live with her. After that, Dad drove to Lake Worth to drop off Barbara to live at Aunt Sadie's and dropped Johnny off at Uncle Joe's. This would be residence number eleven for us. I was ten years old, and Ray was eleven.

This was an almost unbearable time for us. Now everybody was gone except my brother, Ray. I really don't know how I would have handled it if he and I had been separated.

Grandma enrolled Ray and me in a Chicago school named Bass School. They had a unique setup. They had 5A and 5B semesters and the same system carried through all the grades — 5A was the first semester and 5B was the second semester. Since we had flunked the first semester, we were able to take the 5A semester over again, which meant that at the end of the school year we would have only completed the first semester. If we had stayed at that school, we would have taken 5B for one semester and then have gone to 6A. In reality, we were a half year behind where we would have been, had we not flunked.

My dad moved in with Dolly and got a job fairly quickly with a company called Stone Containers. I am not sure how long he worked there before he caught his foot in a press and crushed about every bone in his foot. He had to go on disability, and that put a real damper on being able to save any money. He would come to visit Ray and me on weekends, and we would look forward to seeing him.

Grandma Gallo, sister Dolly
1980s

80

He had kept in touch with Barbara and Johnny by phone, and he would always keep us abreast of how they were doing. Barbara had started school in Florida and Johnny seemed to be doing fine. He had his cousin Bobby to play with. Bobby was Uncle Joe's youngest son, and Ray and I had not met him. He was close to Johnny's age.

Bass School was quite an experience for Ray and me. It was our first experience going to a racially-integrated school. I would guess that the school was about seventy percent white and thirty percent black. That is strictly a guess. I just remember that it was more than fifty percent white. I am trying to be careful here because I am in "politically correct" territory, but in these memoirs, I am trying to be as honest as I know how.

Were Ray and I prejudiced? Absolutely not! We were raised in Ironwood, and I don't ever remember seeing one black person the whole time we lived there. Also, I don't remember anyone ever saying anything bad about a person of color. It is just that the change from Ironwood to an inner-city school in Chicago was staggering.

We were constantly being asked by white and black kids alike: "Where are you guys from? You talk funny!"

Imagine that! We thought they all talked funny! We got along with the kids fairly well, but since we only went to the school for one semester, we didn't have enough time to make good friends.

Ray and I walked to school and back during this time. Living with Grandma was a little hard. She worked a lot and Ray and I were a little rowdy — I am sure we got on her nerves. She and my grandpa had divorced years before, and she had an Italian boy-friend named Frank. He did not live there all the time but would come on weekends and sometimes spend the night. At this time, he and Grandma were probably in their mid-fifties.

Grandma had bought many houses during the depression years and had sold most of them, but she still had a number of houses that she rented out. Frank was a carpenter and most of his time was spent working on Grandma's houses. If anyone knows Chicago, she lived near the corner of 63rd and Laflin.

I am sure Ray and I were an interruption to their plans. I know Grandma loved us and wanted the best for us, but she was busy and stressed to the point that she did not have much patience with two young boys.

Grandma had been talking to my father about us going to live with him. Grandma and my father were still on good terms, and I think she liked him more than Dad. They were both members of the SDA church, and I am sure that had something to do with it. Anyway, they made the decision for Ray and me to go and live with our father, Lester. We had lived with Grandma approximately six or seven months.

It was the summer of 1953, and here we go again. We would be moving to Broadview, Illinois, to live with our father. This would be residence number twelve, and I had just turned eleven years old.

Our childhood years were not going very well. The most inner pain for me was in thinking about my mother. I didn't feel comfortable at my grandma's house, but I did not blame her, not one bit. I missed Barbara, Johnny, and my dad so much. I was eleven years old, and Ray was twelve, and it seemed like nobody loved or wanted us. Anyway, that was my gut feeling at that age.

Little did I know that this hard life I was experiencing was a training ground for my adult life when I had to be strong for my own family. It also helped me understand the needs of a child and what it takes to make them happy.

But back to an eleven-year-old's mentality. Here we go again. *Will we ever be united as a family? How long is this separation going to last?*

My heart was heavy. My dad was not able to do anything about this decision since he was not able to support us. I thought it was ironic that just a year and a half ago my father was denied custody of Ray and me. Now, here we are, moving in with him and Marie. It was not our choice to do this, but then again, we really had no choice in the matter.

We were getting used to being tossed around and people leaving us, but it was still hard. We had begun to realize that we needed to just suck it up and make the best of our situation.

We did have a few things going for us when we moved back to the Field Avenue house. We had met and played with some of the neighborhood kids when we spent part of a summer there with my father and Marie. Our playmates were Kenny and his sister, Judy, who lived across the street, and next door to them was Elaine. Another friend was Art Thompson who lived a block behind us. Right next door to us was Chuck Lawrence.

All of us kids were about the same age and spent a lot of time playing together. Field Avenue was a short dead-end street that ended at a Forest Preserve. We would all venture into it and down the hill to a creek, where we had a lot of fun playing and trying to build something that we would call a boat and ride on it.

We also had another couple of surprises when we moved in. We were introduced to Alfred Pellerin, who was Marie's only child by a previous marriage. Al had just graduated from high school and was getting ready to start college.

We took an instant liking to him. He loved the fact that there were two kids, Ray and me, that he could call his brothers. He would take us everywhere and acted like he was so proud of us. He would introduce us to his friends and say, "This is Ray and Billy; they are my brothers." He would be beaming when he spoke this.

Al would take us to Chicago Cubs baseball games, and once in a while to a Chicago White Sox game when they were playing the New York Yankees. I became a Cubs fan while I was there, but I always liked the Yankees. Back then we could sit in the bleachers at Wrigley Field in Chicago for fifty cents.

Wrigley Field

Al would also take us to a huge swimming pool, and he tried to teach us how to dive. He was an excellent diver and would do double somersaults off of the high dive. He was very athletic. He had a part-time job in the summer, so we could not be with him as much as we would have liked.

We were living in our twelfth residence during our short lifetime, and we weren't through moving by a long shot. It was the summer of 1953, and we had a lot of friends before long. The Field Avenue house was a regular bungalow, but my father and Marie had made the attic into an upstairs apartment that they rented out.

Shortly before we got there, they moved upstairs and rented the main floor to Marie's brother, Marty. Marty and his wife had four children who we became close to. The main floor was larger, so Father and Marie decided to let them have the middle floor, and we would all live in the upstairs apartment.

We were told that this new family — Marty, his wife, and four children — were our uncle, aunt, and cousins. So be it. I didn't understand how that could be since we had just met them and we weren't related to them, but it never was a point of contention.

We really liked the kids. Babe (Marty Jr.) was the oldest and perhaps a year younger than Al. Then there was Madeline. She was our age and pretty as a picture. I had a childhood crush on her, but when I tried to talk to Ray about it, he would say, "She can't be your girlfriend!" I asked him why and he would explain, "Because she is your cousin."

I asked, "Who says?"

He responded, "Everyone says she is your cousin, so she must be." Oh, well, how do you argue with that line of thinking?

Then there was Ginny who was a couple of years younger than us, and Johnny, who was about four or five at the time. It was a pretty fun summer as far as playing outside was concerned. We played badminton, croquet, and whiffle ball in the yard and explored all over the Forest Preserve. This kept us occupied during the day, but that lonely feeling that comes from being separated from your family never did go away.

It was still very hard for me at night. I would lay there and cry out for my mother. No matter how much fun we would be having, I always felt out of place and had this sense of not belonging that hung over me all the time.

Father and my sister, Dolly, did not have a great relationship, and so we didn't often see her. She lived about twenty miles away from us in a neighboring suburb called Blue Island, Illinois. My father, at our constant request, took us to see her and allowed us to spend the night there a few times. We loved that and didn't want to go back to Broadview. But we knew we were not in charge, so we succumbed to the situation.

Sometime during that summer of 1953, we were informed that we would be moving to Berrien Springs, Michigan, for the school year. Marie and her son, Al, were very close and they wanted him to go to Emmanuel Missionary College which was located in Berrien Springs, a small town close to Benton Harbor. The plan was to rent a house there while my father and Marie found jobs for the school year. The object was for Al to be able to stay at home instead of the dormitory. I think that Marie felt like he still needed his mother.

Aunt Gen, sister Barbara

Ray and I were glad he was going to be living with us instead of in the dormitory. He was still a good brother to us and would take us on campus every chance he could. We lived a few miles off campus, and Al was allowed to use the car whenever possible. But sometimes he had to walk.

Emmanuel Missionary College (EMC) was a Seventh Day Adventist institution and had a grade school on campus that Ray and I would attend. We would be starting sixth grade with Mr. Peterson as our teacher. He was also the principal of the school. He was nice, but very firm and to the point.

I actually learned a lot while in sixth grade. We had never played soccer before, but that seemed to be the sport that everyone liked at our school. We were not in a league and did not compete with other schools, but we played each other at every recess, after school, and whenever possible. I really started to like soccer, although I was getting kicked in the shins a lot.

Ray and I joined the grade school tumbling team. That was fun, although neither of us were very good at it. I finally got to the point that I could do a handstand, but if I tried to walk on my hands, it was all over.

Berrien Springs is kind of a neat place. It is in the heart of what they call the "fruit belt." We ate a lot of fruit and also picked plums several times, and Marie canned fruit since it was reasonably priced and plentiful.

Brother Johnny, Ironwood Twp.
1962 — Age 13

I remember going to town with Al quite a few times, and we would see many students who were on their way back to South Bend where they were attending Notre Dame and had decided to stop in Berrien Springs for whatever reason.

Al had just bought a nice school jacket that had the initials EMC on the back of it. One time when we were in town some of the Notre Dame students scoffed at the initials on Al's jacket. "What is EMC? Is it Eggheads, Muffins, and Cornbread?" they would ask. Then they would stand around and laugh and laugh and say it again.

Al would hang his head and not say anything. There were three or four of them. I sure didn't like it, but it gave me an idea of what bullying was all about. I felt sorry for Al and wished there was something I could have done. But that was out of the question since I was only eleven years old.

The house we had moved into had an upstairs apartment that we rented. The landlords, Mr. and Mrs. Block, lived on the main floor. This was the thirteenth place where we had resided. Marie was doing small jobs for people, like ironing and washing clothes and doing some needle work. My father was having some difficulty finding work at first, but finally he got a job as a painter and would be working directly for the college. He would be painting mostly the exteriors of houses that were owned by the university.

As soon as he started working, he discovered that since he worked for the college, he was able to rent one of the houses that the school owned. And being an employee of the school, it would be at a reduced rate. So that is exactly what he did. We would be moving to residence number fourteen. This time we had the whole house to ourselves, although it was fairly small. It was just a few short blocks from campus, so it was an easy walk for us back and forth to school.

Al had met a girl at school that he really liked and he was anxious for Ray and me to meet her. Her name was Coral, and she was staying at the dormitory. He took us over to meet her one weekend and again introduced us as his brothers. Again, he was just beaming. I wondered why it was that he liked us so much. The only thing I can come up with was that he was an only child and had probably always wanted a brother or sister.

Coral seemed to like us and I remember her saying we were cute. They started spending more and more time together as time went on. Eventually they were engaged, and later married. Al and Coral ended up having five children: Bethel, Dawn, Holly, Lisa, and Vernon.

Meanwhile, my dad kept in touch with Ray and me through a series of notes. To this day, I do not remember how he got the notes to us, but he did. In one note he instructed us to go to a certain corner in town where there was a pay phone, and at a certain time he would call us. We managed to do that and we both talked to him for quite a while. He told us that he would be coming to Berrien Springs to see us and what hotel he would be staying at. He instructed us to come there at a certain time on Sunday, and he would be in the lobby waiting for us.

We were able to do that and were so happy to see him. He had some pictures to show us that Uncle Joe and Aunt Sadie had mailed to him of Barbara and Johnny. We were excited to see him, and we all shed a few tears.

He informed us that he would be getting a Workman's Compensation settlement for his injured foot in the near future. And when he did receive it, he was going to Florida to pick up Barbara and Johnny, come to Broadview to pick up Ray and me, and head straight back to Ironwood to live.

Wow! That was great news to us. We were both happy about the news, but it became a waiting game and we did not know how long it would take for all this to come about. We finished our entire sixth grade school year at Berrien Springs before moving back to Broadview.

Al and Coral still had not married at this point, although they had a long-distance relationship, so we would all be living together. Marty's oldest son, Babe, had found a job and moved out, and Marty decided to move from the main floor to upstairs because the rent was cheaper. So, when we moved back, we would be occupying the middle floor which was a lot nicer.

Although it was the same house, I am going to count it as another residence because it was a different apartment. Okay, folks, this will be residence number fifteen. We were back in Broadview for the summer of 1954, and Ray and I were both twelve years old.

We picked up right where we had left off with all our friends. I became very close to Chuck Lawrence who lived next door. Chuck was a year or so older than us, but he had a new bike. He would have me ride on the back. and we would pedal around town. I remember him taking me by bicycle to a fast-food place called Cock Robin to buy me a hamburger. My father and Marie were strict vegetarians, and we never ate meat except when I would go riding with Chuck.

Chuck's father, Charles Lawrence, was a painting contractor, and Chuck always seemed to have spending money. He helped his father in the summer, and I loved the fact that he had money — we didn't have any. He was very generous with his money.

My father never did buy us a bicycle, so Ray and I never had a bicycle that we could call our own for our entire childhood. Summer continued on, and we were anxiously awaiting word from Dad about moving back.

10

Moving Back to Ironwood

OKAY, BACK TO THE STORY. Here we are in Broadview awaiting word from Dad that he had received his Workers' Compensation money. Then he would be picking up Barbara and Johnny in Florida, come by to pick us up in Broadview, and we would all head to Ironwood.

This rocked along for just about the whole summer. We picked up with our friends where we had left off the summer before. We became a little closer to the kids in the neighborhood and spent a great deal of time playing whiffle ball and croquet. I was an avid Chicago Cubs fan and a big Ernie Banks fan. My father would let me go to the Cubs games by myself. He would drop me off in Des Plaines, Illinois, where I would catch what was called the "L" train. I would have to transfer one time before getting off a few blocks from Wrigley Field.

Even though we enjoyed our friends, they did not fill the void that Ray and I felt for our family. Each day seemed like agony when we never heard anything from Dad. Finally, the day came somewhere around the middle of July 1954. Dad knew where we lived, so he drove over to our neighborhood. Ray happened to be down the street riding someone's bicycle. Dad stopped him and said he had received his Workers' Comp settlement, and was leaving for Florida to pick up Barbara and Johnny. He told Ray that he would pick us up in three days on the corner of our street, and he told us what time to be there.

It was fairly early in the morning the best I remember. I was in the back yard when Ray came up to me riding a bicycle. I never did see Dad that day. He left as soon as he talked to Ray. I can't tell you how ecstatic I was when I heard the news. The three-day wait seemed like an eternity.

The day we left, we tried to be careful because we were basically running away, and we did not want Father or Marie to stop us. We did not pack anything, just had the clothes that we had put on that morning. We tried to not act any differently when we got up that morning and ate breakfast as usual. It did not arouse any suspicion when we went outside because that is where we stayed pretty much all the time.

We walked to the corner when it was close to the time that Dad said he would pick us up. We waited and waited. Finally, they came in a black 1951 Buick Century (I think it was a Century, but I know it was a black '51 Buick).

My heart was racing when I saw them; I was so happy. Johnny was standing in the seat next to Dad with a pair of shorts and cowboy boots on, and Barbara was sitting on the passenger seat with her face pressed against the window. Both of them were smiling, and there was a lot of hugging going on when they stopped.

Dad finally said, "Get in the car, and let's get going."

Wow! This was so great. Ray and I jumped in the back seat, and we were off on our way back to Ironwood. The thrill of that day is still burned in my memory bank. Here we were being kidnapped again. Wait! I guess it was not kidnapping since my dad had won custody of us close to three years prior. Anyway we were being stolen (I think). We were all together, except for Ronnie, and it seemed too good to be true.

It had been a little over a year and a half since we had seen Barbara and Johnny. There is no way that siblings should be split up for this long. What an emotional strain it had been. I know now that Dad was trying his best to fulfill the promise he had made to Mother to keep the family together. It would have been easy for him to throw up his hands and leave us in Broadview. Life couldn't be any better than it was right now. All the pain and trauma we had been going through was shoved into the background as we were enjoying these precious moments. We were thinking about our aunts, uncles, cousins, and friends in Ironwood, and we were anxious to see everyone again.

We were getting ready to move into our sixteenth residence when we arrived in Ironwood. This move would be different than the other moves, in that it gave us a degree of stability. We would reside in this house in Ironwood Township for almost five years.

Dad had previously employed a lumberjack named George Koski when Dad and Waiko were doing the big logging job in Wakefield. I remember him from the bunkhouse when Ray and I would go there to be with the lumberjacks and listen to their stories. Some of them played poker while we were visiting, which was almost every night. George was one who didn't play cards, so Ray and I both remembered talking with him. He was a nice man. He owned a house and some acreage on (what is now called) Saari Lane in Ironwood Township. It was called Nyman Road when we moved there. It was probably named after the man who lived at the end of the road, Ted Nyman.

So here we are moving into the old Koski place. There was an old barn, a fairly big shed where some animals could be kept, an outhouse, and a blacksmith shop that still had some old tools in it. There was a well with a pump located about thirty feet from the house. People who are into historic and antique things would probably have been fascinated with it.

George had lost his wife and consequently lost interest in the place. He started drinking heavily and never went back to his home. It was just sitting there empty. I have no idea how long it had been empty, but he obviously had no intention of going back. Anyway, Dad and he worked out some kind of deal where we would be moving into this house.

I don't remember ever seeing George, not one time, even though we lived there for almost five years. I'm pretty sure we didn't pay rent, because somewhere along the line, I would have known about that fact. The house was located quite a distance from the road. I know it was at least the length of a football field. In the winter, I had to carry wood from the road to the house and it seemed like a very long way. There was no possibility of getting to the house in the winter, since no one was available to plow that long driveway. So we had to park the car at the road and walk to the house all winter.

We had electricity, but it was pretty crude. There were no switches for the lights. In order to turn a light on in each room, we had to tighten the bulb, and to turn it off, just loosen the bulb. I don't remember there being any electrical receptacles, but it is possible there were a few. Since we didn't have any appliances to plug in at this point, it didn't matter.

The house was small, containing a kitchen, pantry, living room, and one bedroom. There was an unfinished upstairs with a big flat door with hinges on it that you had to lift to open in order to have access to it. The walls were bare studs with insulation between the studs. There was an old wood stove for cooking and a potbellied stove in the living room for heat. There was no running water in the house, and consequently, there was no indoor plumbing.

The outhouse was located pretty far from the house next to the barn, and that would prove to be a big problem at times. We were totally dependent on wood for cooking and heating.

When we moved in, it was decided that Ray and I would live in the upstairs unfinished room, Barbara would sleep in the living room, and Johnny would stay in the bedroom with Dad. Living conditions in that house were hard at times, especially in the winter. But hey, we were together and we would make the most of it.

We ended up really liking the area we lived in because of our neighbors. Dad's sister, Jenny, and her husband, Alfred Ranta, lived down the road about a quarter mile past our house. The Rantas were our cousins, and we remembered them well because we visited them often. Ray and I would spend the night there when we lived on Curry Street. All of us had been in kindergarten together. That included Arthur and Wesley and our other cousin, Ruthie Spetz, Waiko's daughter. Now all of us would be starting seventh grade at Roosevelt, the same school we all went to in kindergarten.

Across the road lived Arvo (Bubs) and Marian Saari. They had two boys who we often played with. Russell Saari was two years older than us, and his brother, Marvin, was about that much younger than us. They had a daughter named Marlene, but she was a baby or at least pretty young. Before getting to our house, on the right side of the road, were Reino and Sylvia Saari. They had two boys, Johnny and Gary. Reino and Bubs had the same last name, but Marlene informed me that they were not related, and Marian and Sylvia were sisters.

Other close neighbors were Gilman Hill and his sister, Nancy. Then there were the Aaltonens (Levi, Peter, and Ruth). I hope I am not boring everyone with these names, but since I am targeting people who lived in Ironwood, I thought a lot of you would know some of the names I mentioned, even though this was many, many years ago. Bubs Saari would be our bus driver for the entire time we attended Roosevelt. It was kind of neat to realize that your neighbor was your bus driver, and his children were your friends.

Despite the living conditions at the house we were renting, this move to Ironwood Township brought a little stability to our lives. We bounced around a lot before that. During this time we had time to form more lasting relationships than previously, simply because we were there longer.

Ray and I registered for seventh grade at Roosevelt Junior High, while Barbara would be starting second grade, and Johnny would be starting kindergarten under the tutelage of Mrs. Olson, the same teacher we had when we attended kindergarten there. Dad went back to working in the woods with Waiko, but sometimes he would work with other loggers in the area.

Dad now walked with a limp because of the crushed foot he suffered in Chicago. He had a lot of trouble with his feet. He would have me pull off his boots when he got home, and, believe me, that was a chore. His feet would be swollen and it was very difficult to pull off the boots. I remember several times pulling so hard that my hands would slip and I would go flying across the floor. Dad would grimace with pain the whole time. It was not a pleasant thing to do, but it had to be done, and he couldn't manage it himself. Arthritis had also started to settle into his damaged foot, and some arthritis started showing up in the joints of his fingers.

There was one thing that kept this from being one of the happiest times in our life, and that was our brother, Ronnie. He was always in my thoughts. Mother had given her life having him, and we couldn't even see him. That thought plagued my mind constantly. Dad had talked to Mrs. Jones about paying her. The problem was that he had gotten so far behind in his payments that he didn't have all the money needed to catch up. He tried to give her a partial payment and work something out about catching up with the balance later. She wasn't hearing any of that. It was obvious that she had no plans of giving up Ronnie.

Looking back, I understand that. She naturally got attached to him because she had him since he was a very small baby, and he was close to three years old now. This ended up being the last time he talked to her. I believe she was in fear of us kidnapping Ronnie or perhaps losing him in a custody battle. She turned hostile, as anyone probably would, if someone was trying to take their loved one away.

After the proposal concerning the money Dad owed her, she forbade him to ever come to her house again. She wanted to cut all ties with our family, and that included us.

Later that year, just before Christmas, Dad had bought Ronnie (Ronald Charles) some nice Christmas presents and decided, since she would not let him in, he would drive to her house and stay in the car while Ray and I brought the presents up the back steps and hopefully get to see our brother. I was so nervous that I was probably shaking. Ray and I had tried to see him when we lived on Ridge Street, and I remember that encounter very well. Dad never did know about it because we were afraid to tell him. I was hoping somehow she might have softened since the last time.

So, here Ray and I go again. The back steps were kind of treacherous, just like before. They had crusty ice on them and I figured they never used them. If you are wondering why we didn't go to the front door, all I can say is, "I am wondering the same thing." The side of their house faced the front of our house when we lived on Ridge Street, and it was a lot closer.

As Ray knocked on the door, I knew my heart had to be beating a hundred miles an hour. Just like before, Mrs. Jones didn't come right away, so Ray does a repeat performance of the other time we were there. He banged on the door like he was trying to knock the house down. *Holy cow!* I thought for sure something would fall off the house the way he was banging. "Stop!" I hollered.

He just stepped back and said, "That will get their attention."

Yeah, right! Here I am about to jump out of my skin, and he is acting like he is going to knock the house down.

He was right, as it didn't take very long and Mrs. Jones came to the door with a very angry look on her face. "What do you want?" she blurted.

I hadn't rehearsed my answer so I bluntly said, "We are Ronnie's brothers and we would like to give these presents to him." I'm sure I probably stuttered a little because I was very nervous.

I will never forget what she said. "Just put the presents on the steps. You are not coming in, and you are not going to see Ronnie. Don't ever come back again."

We were crushed. *How could she be so cruel?* I thought. *He is our brother, and how is it that she can tell us we can't see him?* It is only as I got older that I began to understand. Mother was gone and our family was falling apart. Ronnie was actually better off than we were. Quite naturally, he didn't remember Mother or any of us, so he would not ever go through the pain that we felt during these years.

When we got back to the car where Dad was anxiously waiting, he asked, "What did she say?" I told him exactly what happened. His reply was not very pleasant, to say the least. None of us had seen Ronnie since he was a small baby when Dolly left. Now he was approximately three years old. Ray would never see him again, period. Barbara and I would not see him until he was in his late fifties, and that story would be too long to interject at this point.

With Johnny it was a different story. The three of us had left home and Johnny continued to live in Ironwood Township with Dad. He attended Luther L. Wright, and when Johnny started his junior year, Ronnie started his freshman year. Now they would both be in the same school for the next two years.

You would think that would work out great, and they would get to know each other. Not to be. Johnny was a really tough football player and very strong and aggressive. He played on the only undefeated football team the Ironwood Red Devils had ever had — or maybe the last undefeated team — and led the team in tackles. Plus, he had won an All-State Honorable Mention.

Ronnie was afraid of him. The first time Johnny approached him at school, Ronnie quickly went the other way. In fact, he took measures to make sure he wouldn't have to face Johnny. Of course, Johnny was heartbroken. Dad remained depressed about the whole situation also. He thought perhaps Johnny and Ronnie would develop a relationship that would enable him to see his son again.

Now back to the time frame when we were getting ready to start seventh grade. Dad had contacted his attorney to see if he

7th grade boys; Bill is at far right

could get Ronnie back. I don't know what they talked about, but I do know the case never came to court.

It wasn't long after that when some people from Children's Services — or whatever they called it — came over to our house, talked to all of us, and checked out the house. That was the last thing I know about the custody situation, and Dad never said another word about it to us.

When I got older, I realized the decision was a no-brainer. Ronnie was better off where he was. Mrs. Jones had Ronnie three years already, our mother had passed away, and our living conditions were substandard compared to where he was. Mrs. Jones had a husband who was a retired railroad worker, and so they were able to offer Ronnie some stability. However, that didn't mean that it made it any easier. It was almost like my mother and Ronnie died at the same time. The decision meant that our relationship would continue to be totally cut off. I will repeat what I said earlier: **The mother is the adhesive that holds the family together.** The loss of my mother and the loss of Ronnie have haunted me all my life, even to this day. Ronnie finished college and was a book publisher for a long time, and later worked for Microsoft.

Our home life was not very bad in the summer, even though we had no bathroom or running water, no place to take a bath or shower, no telephone, no radio, and no television for sure. I remember when, as a young man years later, one of my friends in the Chicago area asked me if I wanted to go camping with them. They explained that the place where they were going had no bathrooms, so you just had to find yourself a spot in the woods. There was no water, except for a spring down at the foot of a nearby hill. Also, in order to cook you had to get a fire started. He and his brother did not know about my past when they asked me, "Do you think you can handle it?"

Handle it? I had camped out for at least five years straight — spring, summer, fall, and winter. I thanked them for asking me, but I told them I would pass. At this time I had just rented a furnished apartment with James Key, a friend I had met at work.

It was not long after we moved in that this request to go camping came. I was close to eighteen at this time. *Nope!* No camping for me. I was just getting used to these luxuries. I loved it when I turned on a switch and the light came on. It was like magic. All I had to do now was turn a handle — no pumping — and water came pouring out.

No building a fire to have hot water. It came out of a faucet, too. If we were cold or hot, we only had to turn a dial. No walking out in the hot summer or freezing winter to use the outhouse. Just push down on a handle and everything disappeared. Turn a handle and the gas cook stove came on. Before I left Ironwood, I had never taken a shower in a house. The only shower I had ever taken was in a locker room environment at school. Now we had a tub and shower of our own, inside the house! Folks, I was living the life of luxury. It couldn't be any better than this. *Camping?* You've got to be kidding me.

Okay, back to Ironwood Township and the Roosevelt School years. Like I said, summer was not bad at all. There were some high points. For the most part, I stayed home and did chores and helped with Barbara and Johnny. I would feed the animals, light fires, chop wood, haul water, and help wash and hang out clothes.

Brother Ray
in 7th grade

Ray went to work in the woods with Dad and Waiko. I would go periodically, when they needed help with pulp wood. I would help guide the pulp as it was placed on a truck with a hoist and then ride to Bessemer and help guide it into train cars for shipment. The best I can remember, Ray lived at home the year we were in seventh grade, but then moved in with Waiko to help Ruthie on the farm. He continued to work in the woods in the summer and some weekends.

I cannot imagine being any unhappier than I was at this point. It was like my whole world was crumbling. My fondest memories of working at this time were helping our neighbors during haymaking season. I remember helping Ted Nyman for several years, along with the Aaltonens, and Eric Lehikoinen. This was great. Bringing hay in from the fields is hard work, but we always looked forward to lunch. The lady of the house went all out at haymaking time, and the food was delicious. During this time I was introduced to *kallia*, which is Finnish for homemade root beer.

Here is the best part. They not only served these wonderful meals, which were ten times better than anything we could expect at home, but they also gave us money. It was one of the few times I had money of my own. We were paid fifty cents an hour. Before you think that was not much money, think about the fact that a candy bar cost five cents and we could buy ten of them for fifty cents. We could buy three gallons of gas for close to fifty cents.

I joined the 4H club in the Township, and I really enjoyed it. I remember taking a course in gun safety, which was helpful when I went into the woods one time to deer hunt. Another highlight was that all of us young teenagers were in a Dairy Judging contest. We had been studying about cows and what to look for when judging them on appearance.

We all came together at Kenny Vuorenmaa's farm in Ironwood Township to compete with one another on our ability to judge cows. They lined up five cows on the side of the barn and gave us each a sheet of paper. We were asked to write down which cow we ranked number one in appearance, and list all the reasons why, and then second, and so on through number five. There were probably fifteen or so kids involved, and I was fortunate enough to win.

A little later, I received a letter inviting me to be a dairy judge at the Upper Peninsula State Fair in Escanaba, Michigan. The panel of judges were all adults, except for me. I would represent the 4H club for the UP. I was ecstatic! I was going to be somebody! Imagine me being a judge representing the 4H club for the Upper Peninsula of Michigan. Whoa!

In the letter, however, was the question: *Can you be there at a certain time and date?* I had to reply within a certain time frame. If I couldn't make it, they would get someone else. I tried really hard to be able to go. I talked to Dad and he said we just didn't have the money. Someone would have to drive me to Escanaba plus bring me back, and I would need money for food. I don't remember what the sleeping arrangements would be, but suffice it to say, no one was able to help me. So I could not go.

Winter time was often brutal for us. We depended entirely on wood for our survival, and it was a staggering chore to stay ahead of the game. Dad never made wood for the winter. He would come home with a load of wood in his car trunk, as needed. It was cut to length, but it wasn't split. That was my job after school. If the pieces were too heavy to handle, I would get an axe and split them by the road before carrying them to the house. Many times this was done after dark.

Mornings were tough in the winter. Just imagine waking up in the morning and it being so cold in the house that you could see your breath. Walking on a cold floor would make your feet feel like icicles. It was my job to stoke the fire and put some dry wood on it to get it burning and get some heat in the house. Fast-burning wood was not always available. Dad would usually get the kitchen fire going and put the coffee water on. Back then, we boiled the coffee in a pot and strained it into our cup.

Getting ready for school was extremely difficult. We would do our best to heat some water in time to use a wash basin to clean up for school. When we were at Roosevelt, the bus came right past our house, but later when we went to Luther L. Wright High School, we had to walk about a mile to meet the bus.

If memory serves me correctly, our local radio station, WJMS, carried the Detroit Tigers baseball games during our first year at Roosevelt, which would have been 1954-55. I loved listening to the Tigers games and had been a Tigers fan since childhood.

I had also become a Cubs fan in Chicago, but the Cubs were in the National League, and the Tigers were in the American League. We did not have a radio that year, but I did get to listen to some of the games on the car radio. Also in my memory bank is tucked away the fact that WJMS quit carrying the Tigers games the following year and started carrying the Milwaukee Braves games (now the Atlanta Braves).

I was disappointed because it was this year that we finally got a radio and I was looking forward to listening to the Tigers games. This is where my friend, Russell Saari, helped out. He had a radio that picked up the Tigers games on another station, but the reception only came in clear enough if we were in the milk house. We ended up spending hour after hour listening to the games in the milk house.

I was also an Ironwood Red Devils fan, but couldn't attend the games because of our financial situation. I think I managed to make it to a couple of games. That is when I came to appreciate Bob Olson, who I think started broadcasting the Red Devils

Van Patrick

football games live in 1955. He was my hero. I really liked Van Patrick who did the Tigers games back then, but I thought Bob Olson was every bit as good as him, and maybe even better. Bob had a way of making the games exciting. He made me feel like I was right there.

I was especially interested that year because some of the Roosevelt football team, who were now sophomores, were on the team. David Landretti (Buckshot) was the starting fullback.

Buckshot was the star on the undefeated team that Roosevelt had the year before. He made the starting lineup for the Red Devils in his sophomore year after graduating from Roosevelt Junior High. I would get so excited when Bob would say something to this effect: "Landretti up the middle, dragging would-be tacklers with him down to the 40 — 45 — 50 yard line — first down! This David Landretti is one strong kid."

Some years later, after I moved to Illinois, I would come back often to visit. On a certain Friday, we had left the Chicagoland area heading to Ironwood. This was somewhere around 1966, and my brother, Johnny, was on the team that went undefeated that year. As we got close to Ironwood, I turned on WJMS, and the Red Devils had just won another game. Bob Olson was interviewing my brother, Johnny, who had led the team in tackles. I couldn't believe it! Here was my favorite announcer of all time interviewing my brother and congratulating him. I cannot tell you how happy I was at that moment.

Bob Olson

Let me fast forward to just a short time ago. I was on a Hurley, Wisconsin, Facebook page, when a lady mentioned she was Bob Olson's daughter. Folks, that got my attention. I loved Bob Olson. Anyway, I never did know what had happened to Bob and often had wondered about him. His daughter, Rosana, informed me that he had passed away a year or so ago. I felt so sad. I would give anything if I could hear him broadcast one more game. RIP Bob!

11

The Roosevelt Years: Part 1

THE ROOSEVELT YEARS COVER THE period from 1954, when we started seventh grade at Roosevelt Junior High School, until 1957, when we graduated after finishing ninth grade. We had a lot of fun in the summer of 1954, including swimming at Spring Creek, just down the road from the Haanpa's house where Donny, Margie, and Royce lived. We also played softball, either in the Saari's front yard or ours.

We really got to know our Ranta cousins a lot better since they lived just down the road from us. The two sets of Ranta twins would ride the school bus with Ray and me while we attended Roosevelt. Art and Wes were in the same grade as Ray and me, and Margaret and Marie were one year younger. The other Ranta children, Pat, Joey,

Cousins Art and Wesley Ranta

and Kathy were younger, with Pat being closer to Barbara's age and Joey being closer to Johnny's age. Kathy was the baby. She was so cute with her pretty blond hair. Everybody adored her. The nice thing about it was that they lived within easy walking distance of our house.

Dad and Waiko did a few projects together when we first moved there. They had bought a big workhorse named Queenie to skid logs out of the woods, especially where it was hard to get a dozer in and also where it was really muddy. They had built her a little shed in the woods to stay in at night. When they finished the project, Dad brought her home to our house and we put her in the big shed. She never worked again. She became a big pet. That horse could eat a lot and absolutely loved oats. Feeding Queenie was one of my many chores, and most of the time I liked doing it.

Dad had some kind of deal with Lutey's Green House in downtown Ironwood, where he furnished them with cedar and balsam boughs. Ray and I would go into the woods periodically, and with a knife and small axe, cut small limbs off the trees We put them in bundles of about fifty pounds, and Dad would deliver the bundles to Lutey's where he was paid by the pound.

This continued until I left Ironwood. When I started driving, Ray and I would pick the greens, bundle them, take them to Lutey's, and bring the money home to Dad. Sometimes Dad would pick the greens and later Barbara helped. This was not an everyday job, and I would guess it happened once every two weeks.

Now it was time to start school. Our homeroom teacher in seventh grade was Mrs. Jezek. I am going to name the teachers I can remember at the Junior High level. A lot of you will remember some of them. Besides Mrs. Jezek, there was Mr. Torro, Mr. Mattson (who later became the principal), Mr. Nelmark, Mr. Brown, Mr. Pallin, Mrs. Ekstrom, Mrs. Olson, Mrs. Simpson, and later Mrs. Burla, who taught music. There was also Ken Wiele, the music teacher.

Mrs. Jezek, Homeroom 7th Grade

When I was in ninth grade, I joined the school choir and also a mixed ensemble with Mrs. Burla as the teacher. I really loved her. She was nice and I got vibes from her thinking that she really cared about me. At this point in my life, I was really starved for affection.

The one story that I am going to tell is about Mrs. Burla, and it continues even to the writing of these memoirs. Our music group was getting ready to do a concert and all the boys were supposed to wear white shirts. Well, I didn't have a white shirt and we were dirt poor. I asked Mrs. Burla if it would be all right if I just wore a regular shirt since I didn't have a white one. She said something to the effect of, "I'll get back to you."

Benevolent music teacher, Mrs. Burla

It wasn't long before she called me to the side and said she had something for me. She handed me a nice white shirt and said, "Here you go, Bill." I noticed a tear in her eye and my heart melted. That little tear told me that she knew what I was going through, and she cared enough to help me. This one act of kindness has stayed with me my entire life, and I have never forgotten it. The time frame was probably 1956-57.

Okay, are you ready for this story to carry over to 2017? Some sixty years later, when I had been writing and placing stories in a couple of Ironwood Facebook groups, I noticed one person who responded had the last name of Burla. I messaged her and asked if she was related to Mrs. Burla, the music teacher. She replied that she was her daughter-in-law and that Mrs. Burla was ninety years old and still directing music for a church.

I asked the lady if she would ask her mother-in-law if she remembered me. I really did not expect that she did. I didn't say one word about the shirt. She responded later and said Mrs. Burla remembered a Spetz kid who didn't have a white shirt for a concert. I was stunned. She remembered this one incident, as I did, sixty years later. Yes, that choked me up. I told her to tell Mrs. Burla that I love her for what she did way back then. She later contacted me again and said that Mrs. Burla was telling everybody that this incident just made her Christmas. God bless you, Mrs. Burla.

Mr. Brown,
assistant football
coach and
science teacher

When I was in seventh grade, Roosevelt Junior High had the best football team it ever had. Although I was too young and small to be on the team, I did, however, watch all the home games as they either were undefeated or lost one game.

The team was outstanding, and I can remember some of the players, although most were two years older than me. Russell Saari, our neighbor, was the quarterback. David Landretti (Buckshot) was the star of the team and played fullback.

Buckshot was six feet tall and weighed two hundred pounds, which was big for a fourteen-year-old freshman in junior high school. He was an "up the middle" type runner, and would drag would-be tacklers with him many times as he crossed the goal line. The following year when he left Roosevelt and attended Luther L. Wright High School, he was the starting fullback as a sophomore on the varsity football team.

I also remember Roland Nelson and Donny Haanpaa, who played in the line, and Ronald Saari, who was a halfback on Roosevelt's winning team.

We had the weirdest nicknames while we were at Roosevelt. For instance, Russell Saari's nickname was *Rat Hole*. How strange is that? Not Rat, but *Rat Hole*. Since most of my classmates were of Finnish descent, I was one of the very few kids who had black hair. My friend, Ed Gullan, named me *Black One*, not Blackie or even Black, but *Black One*. That name stayed with me for the entire three years I was at Roosevelt. I did talk to a couple of the kids when they were doing the yearbook and asked them to not use the nickname *Black One* under my picture in the *Roosette*. They consented and my nickname (just for the book) was Blackie. Ray and I attended all the home games and loved it.

There were several incidents during our three years at Roosevelt that I would like to cover — some bad, and some good. Roosevelt had hot lunches for all the kids, and I really looked forward to them. Some of us would hang around after everyone was finished, and the cooks were happy to give us all the leftovers we wanted.

104

Can you believe we actually had venison sometimes? My favorite food was mashed potatoes and hamburger gravy. There was a small fee for these lunches that the students were expected to pay. I don't remember what it was, but twenty-two cents rings a bell.

So anyway, one day I was called into the principal's office. On my way there I was wracking my brain to see if I could think of anything that I might have done wrong lately. Maybe they found out, whatever it was. Until this day, I cannot believe this happened. I sat down in the principal's office while he stood behind his desk, looked at me very sternly, and said, "Your father is way behind on paying his lunch money. We are going to have to do something about it. You need to talk to him. We have sent him letters, and he doesn't respond. This is serious."

I was speechless. I might have said okay or something, but I walked out of there stunned. I could see their point because there were four of us kids and it probably was a good sum of money. But I was already suffering with low esteem and this was just like somebody stepped on me, like I was an ant. I was thinking that this would probably be the last time we would be able to eat in the cafeteria. I was thirteen years old at the time, and I was perplexed as to what to do.

On the way home I made a decision to not tell Dad. He had a bit of a temper, and I knew this would set him off. I never did say anything to him. I couldn't understand why they talked to me. I didn't owe the money, but I would have paid it if I had it. This is the first time I have ever mentioned this incident. I just don't think it should have been handled this way. I never did find out how it was resolved, but I do know that we continued to eat in the cafeteria at lunchtime.

It was probably in the summer between seventh and eighth grade when Dad and Waiko made some kind of deal to have Ray go and live with Uncle Waiko. He was going to help our cousin Ruthie, who was our age, with milking the cows and doing other chores around his farm.

Uncle Waiko was very busy, but he was fun to be around. He would tell us stories about when he was in World War II and about his exploits as a boxer when

Cousin Ruthie Spets

he was in the military. Logging was only one of the many interesting things that he did.

In addition to being a dairy farmer, he was the ABS Sales Representative in our area, which meant he artificially bred cows. This was new to the area at that time, and it went over well. It meant that farmers no longer had to keep a bull around all year and feed it. For a small fee, Uncle Waiko would come and artificially breed the farmer's cows. I remember going to the train station with him one time to pick up frozen semen for his work. I also watched him artificially breed a few cows, and trust me, it was not a pretty sight.

Brother Ray

It was a devastating blow to me when Ray moved in to live with Uncle Waiko. My brother, my lifelong companion and best friend, was taken away from me. That left me, Barbara, and Johnny at home. The only consolation was that I would see Ray at school every day during the week and then later at football practice, starting in the eighth grade. It was not the same as being with him at home. I really looked forward to school during these years because it was warm there with food to eat — plus Ray was there, along with my cousins and friends. I fell in love with Roosevelt.

Although I loved Roosevelt, there were still issues at home that brought a lot of sadness to me at that age. I was going to school with an attitude problem. I felt like nobody cared for me, which gave me very low self-esteem. Add to that the fact that we were very poor. I think Dad may have worked for maybe three years or so before he became unable to work. When he was working, we ate well, but there never seemed to be any money left for much else.

We had an old Plymouth that kept breaking down. Back then you were lucky to get 100,000 miles on a car, so I imagine that took some of the money. At one point I only had two pairs of pants and two shirts. One of the pairs of pants had a rip in the knee. That was before it was fashionable to have tears in your pants. I was really self-conscious about this.

I hesitate to write this next statement because I know how crazy it is going to sound, but *I actually didn't like kids who had mothers.* I thought they were sissies. I know that sounds childish, and it is. The real reason was that I was jealous because they had a mother, and I did not. I did, however, get along with most of the kids despite getting into fights with some of them. My best friend back then was Jerry Kimble. Because his mother had also died and he was being raised by his dad, I felt a kinship to him.

Another thing that happened in ninth grade that I consider on the upside was that I was elected President of the Student Council and Vice President of our homeroom. After the yearbook was made, I was kicked off both jobs for getting caught smoking in the school building. Fortunately, it was too late for me not to be in the *Roosette*. So, if anyone has one from 1957, there I am in two places.

STUDENT COUNCIL MEMBERS (JUNIOR HIGH SCHOOL)
L — R: Vice-president, Sandra Bolich; President, Bill Spetz;
Mr. Nelmark; Secretary, Margie Haanpaa; Treasurer, Edward Gullan

Another act of kindness came from Mrs. Ekstrom. She was our ninth grade English teacher and was stern. You didn't dare act up in her class. She ran a tight ship, but she loved her students. When it came time to graduate, she stopped me on my way out of her English class and said she wanted to talk to me. I don't know how she knew I didn't have any clothes, but I thought maybe Mrs. Burla had talked to her.

Mrs. Ekstrom,
English teacher with
a big heart

She asked me if I had any dress clothes for graduation. When I told her I didn't, she produced a whole suit and gave it to me. It was the jacket, pants, shirt, and tie. She asked me to go to the restroom, put it on, and come back. She had some pins and after a while she had it all pinned up to take home and alter it. Also, like Mrs. Burla, she did so with tears in her eyes. That really moved me. Needless to say, it shot Mrs. Ekstrom right to the top of the list of my favorite teachers that included Mrs. Burla.

Mrs. Ekstrom also cried at graduation. She was close to her students, especially the girls. I remember hearing she cried at every graduation because she knew she would never see a lot of the students again. Years later when I was in Ironwood, I tried to look her up to thank her, but she was out of town. Then some years after that, I tried again and found she had passed away. It is amazing how much influence a teacher can have on a child.

I can honestly say that I liked every teacher I ever had, and that includes a few who roughed me up a little bit. I knew I had it coming, for sure. I sure didn't go home and tell Dad what happened. That was the day and age when parents stood behind teachers, and telling parents was not a wise thing to do. In today's world, the teachers have been greatly hampered in trying to maintain discipline in the classroom. The students, knowing the new laws prohibit teachers from even touching them, take advantage of that fact, in some cases. Thus, the teacher's role as an authority figure has been greatly diminished.

I graduated third, with no award, out of a class of sixty. Robert Hansen was Valedictorian and Laverne Niemi was Salutatorian. I never took a book home and have always regretted that. I paid attention in class and tried to do all of my work in Study Hall. There were a few tests where I know I could have done better if I had studied at home.

Another thing on the upside was that we were in a basketball league in the Resettlement area of Ironwood. When I say we, I am talking about kids my age mostly. It was intramural, and we played at the gym in the Resettlement. I am not sure about the exact time frame. I believe I was in my last year at Roosevelt.

We had won a few games and lost a few, but there was one team that was undefeated and that team was called "The Old Timers." They were all grown men and included Mr. Torro and Mr. Brown. All the other teams were kids. I don't know how far we were in the season, but they were undefeated. It wasn't that we couldn't run circles around them, we could. The reason they won is because they were smarter than us. They passed the ball around better and took good shots. Think about it. Two of them were former coaches! When we played them, it was a night where it seemed I couldn't miss a shot. We beat them, and I got my name in the paper for scoring thirty points. I clipped it out of the Ironwood *Daily Globe* and carried it in my billfold for a long time.

Another exciting thing that happened was that Dad took me deer hunting for the first time when I was fourteen. Ray was staying with Waiko at the time. We had practiced shooting several days before, and I was ready and very excited. This would be my first time ever to go deer hunting. I had heard so many stories about hunting deer, and now I was going to be a hunter. Wow!

This was the first day of hunting season. We hunted off Moore Road, not too far from where we lived. There was a light snow falling, which is good for tracking deer, and we entered the woods just as daylight was breaking.

Dad noticed some deer tracks that he said were fresh because there was not much snow covering them. After we followed the trails for a little while, we stopped and Dad asked me to stand behind a tree and watch back down the trail from where we had just come. He said sometimes when you are tracking a deer, they make a big circle and start following you. He said he was going to continue tracking, but wanted me to stay there, be quiet, and just keep watching back down the trail.

Sure enough! After watching for what seemed like maybe an hour or less, here comes a buck running up the trail from where we had just come. I don't know if it saw me or perhaps just sensed danger, but it sure put on the brakes abruptly and was just standing there looking in my direction.

I took aim and fired. The deer ran into the woods and was gone, I thought. I walked up the trail where the deer had been standing, and I was convinced that I didn't hit it. I looked in the direction that the deer had gone and didn't see anything.

It wasn't long before Dad showed up. He had heard the shot. I was standing there looking dejected. I couldn't believe I had missed that big buck. I had a wide-open shot. No brush in the way, no nothing, just a clean shot.

He asked me what had happened, and I told him that I had seen a buck and had a good shot and missed. He then asked me where the deer was standing when I shot. I showed him and he carefully inspected the ground and noticed a small spot of blood.

We then followed the tracks for maybe a short twenty feet and there was a fallen tree on the ground that we had to step over to keep tracking. As soon as we stepped over the fallen tree, there was the deer, and it was dead. What happened was that I had taken a frontal shot, and the deer must have turned at the instant that I shot, because the bullet had penetrated the deer's heart right behind the front shoulder.

That was the last time I ever hunted. Nobody told me that a deer dies with its eyes wide open. When I first saw it, I felt sick to my stomach thinking that this was a beautiful animal, and I killed it.

I do not condemn the killing of deer. In fact, I think it is something that must be done in order to keep the deer population under control, and they also provide food. I don't have any problem eating venison either. I just decided then and there that I would leave the killing part to people who loved the sport of hunting.

The Ironwood radio station, WJMS, used to announce the names of the people who had gotten their bucks, how many points (antler points that help to determine weight and age), and how much it weighed; My buck was eight points and weighed two hundred pounds. I never heard my name personally, but I know it was announced because quite a few people told me that they heard the news and were surprised how big my buck was. I lavished in the compliments.

Here is another wrinkle about my attitude when I attended Roosevelt. Most of us who lived in the Township considered the kids who lived in the Resettlement as rich. For the most part, they dressed better than we did, and their houses were a lot newer and nicer than the houses in the Township. I realize now that it wasn't that they were rich; most were average middle-class working people. It's just that a lot of us were so poor that they appeared rich by comparison.

It is funny how that carries over. When I started Luther L. Wright in my sophomore year, the feeling was that all of us kids from the Township, now including the Resettlement kids, thought of the kids who lived in town as rich. How a person dresses in school makes a big statement about their financial status, as most of us perceived it. Kids who didn't have nice clothes (like us) always felt inferior.

Not too many years ago, I finished a five-year stint on the school board of a private school here in Chattanooga. The kids wore uniforms and the subject came up about changing this requirement. I voted to keep it, and although the vote was close, I was in the narrow majority. I like the uniform idea because nobody can overdress anyone, which takes wearing clothes as a status symbol out of the equation.

It seemed sadness and drama just followed me around like a plague. Ray was a really good worker and very strong as a kid, so Dad and Waiko started using him in the woods. That elevated me to "chief cook and bottle washer." When Dad was still working, I had many chores to do. When I came home from school, the fire in the wood cook stove was always burned out. I had to restart the fire so I could put the potatoes on. Our staple food was mashed potatoes. It didn't matter what else we ate, there was always mashed potatoes.

Interestingly enough, in the North, potatoes are considered a staple food. Not so down South. Their staple food is pinto beans. I think I have a handle on that one. Potatoes are one of the vegetables that can be grown in the North in their short growing season.

We always seemed to have some chickens around that I had to feed. No hens, just roosters. Periodically, we would kill and eat one. I did not like the roosters. They were always in attack mode waiting for me to go to the well and get water, and then they would come after me.

Roosters do not have any sense, really. They are not afraid of people, even though we are ten times bigger than they are. They definitely can put the hurt on you if you don't watch them closely and fend them off. I carried a big stick with me when I went to the well just to keep them from getting to me. Sometimes they would give up and walk away, but not often.

Then there was Queenie, the big retired workhorse that was just there for us to take care of. She was a pet — a really big one. We all liked her, but she never did anything but eat. One year we had two Jersey calves that we bought to raise through the summer with the hope of fattening them up a bit and selling them in the fall so we didn't have to keep them in the winter. They were both females and they were twins. We named them Connie and Corrine.

I belonged to the local 4H club and decided to enter Connie in competition at the Gogebic County Fair. I would practice leading her around with a rope and taught her to stop and go on command, turn right or left, turn all the way around, and go back in the other direction. I wound up winning a blue ribbon with her. Then we had a Collie dog named Tinker that I was responsible for feeding. I loved that dog, and he followed me everywhere I went.

The County Fair! *Yes! Yes!* We waited for it all year. It was the premier event in Gogebic County, in my humble opinion. Everybody attended and if you were there most of the time you wound up seeing all your friends, classmates, and neighbors. I loved it. The year I entered Connie in competition, we stayed there all night, two nights in a row. Other kids who had animals at the fair also stayed all night. We just bedded down in a hay pile inside the barn.

The carnival was there also. We had been told by some other kids that if we got up early in the morning and went over to the rides, we could find all kinds of change that had fallen out of the pockets of people while they were riding some of the wilder rides. So that is what we did, and they were right! We found a lot of change and everybody was excited. We put it in a little pile, counted it, and then split it among us. It probably wasn't that much money, but it was enough to get us all excited. If a kid found a quarter, he would scream, and the hunt was on. We were practically running over one another in hopes of finding more change.

Another thing that happened, that I thought long and hard about mentioning because it is kind of embarrassing, was a fight that I had one of the nights when we were at the fair all night. The kids hung around in small groups as we would wander all over the place. There were always three or four of us who hung together.

So, one night we were all in the barn, and I spotted this kid who was a little chunky and a lot shorter than I was. He was with two other kids. I thought this kid would be a perfect target to start a fight with because I was pretty sure I could take him, plus there were more of us than there were of them. This seemed like the perfect time to show off and show all my friends how tough I was (the mentality of an idiot, right?).

The kid wasn't bothering anybody, and I started taunting him and trying to induce him into a fight. I called him names and wound up shoving him around as he was backing up and asking me to just leave him alone because he didn't want to fight. So now I was calling him sissy, chicken, etc. I was sure I had my bluff on him because he was acting like he was scared of me.

Yes, I know. Typical bully. This just made me have more confidence.

I finally got the nerve to slap him across the face. Big mistake! Did I say *big mistake?* Yes, I did. He charged me like a runaway bull. I figured he was going to hit me, so I kept my hands up.

Did he hit me with his fists? Nope! He just kept his head down low and drove his head into my stomach.

Down I went. He had completely knocked the wind out of me. I was done. So now I was lying on the ground holding my stomach.

What a nice kid! He could have jumped in and done a number on me because I was pretty much immobilized, but he didn't. When he saw me on the ground groaning, he just backed off and said something like, "I told you to leave me alone."

I was now wishing I would have.

I cannot really put into words how embarrassed I was. I was out to prove how tough I was, and this shorter, heavyset kid just put me out of commission.

My friends helped me to my feet, and I finally got my breath back and immediately started making excuses. I said things like, "He kind of cheated because I thought we were going to box and he changed it to a wrestling match. Had I known that, I could have prepared for it." *Blah, Blah, Blah.*

When a person has an ego problem it is hard to humble yourself and say, "That served me right." The kid wasn't bothering me and I had picked a fight and lost. Maybe I learned my lesson to stop trying to be a bully.

Did I say that? No! Should I have? *Yes!*

That was pretty much the end of my career of being a bully. Loneliness and depression set in like never before. I would lie in bed many nights and hardly sleep at all. Thoughts of my mother, my sister, and now Ray ran through my head constantly. Sometimes at night I just started shaking and it would take a long time to stop. I would shed tears until I didn't have any left, and then finally fall asleep.

In the morning I would usually have a headache from not getting enough sleep, but I would still have to get up and stoke the fire in the wintertime because it had burned down. It usually had enough hot coals in it that I could just put more wood in it and get it going.

12

The Roosevelt Years: Part 2

SINCE MY BROTHER RAY WAS staying with Waiko, he was only about one mile or less from the football field, and he would meet us there. Probably the best players on our team were Ray and Donny Saari. Ray was the biggest and strongest kid on the team, and Donny Saari was the fastest. Harold Torro was our coach, and I had a great deal of respect for him. He was very much to the point when he felt like he needed to discipline any of the kids.

I remember we were scrimmaging in practice one day, and I got upset with one of the kids and used a little profanity. Coach Torro looked at me and said, "Billy, go take a shower." So I left the field for the locker room knowing full well the reason. That is all he ever said. He never talked to me about it later when the rest of the team hit the locker room, but I figured that it would be best if I didn't talk like that again, and I never did.

We didn't have a very good football team because we were too small. I think we

Coach Harold Torro

Brother Ray

won one game and lost six. The highlight to the season for me was when we played the Ironwood Red Devils freshmen from Luther L. Wright High School. They were the biggest team on our schedule. Eric Kangas, who played right end and called the plays, called a play for Ray to run up the middle in the hole between me and Jack Enberg, who was playing center.

We were able to open the line enough for him to get through, and I remember his shoulder pad hitting mine as he went through. He cut left and headed to the sideline where a couple of tacklers had a shot at him. He just stiff-armed them, and he was gone. Touchdown! We lost the game, but it stands out as a highlight of the season, and we played them twice. This game was on their field, and the second one was on our field. We lost both games. I can remember the names of three of the kids on their team. One was Bill Kurta, who played end, and George Albert, who was a running back. Another player I remember was Tom Bednar.

One day, my cousin Art Ranta hurt his leg in practice and had been sitting on the sidelines in pain. Coach Torro was busy with the other players, so I walked over to Art and told him that he should walk it off, because that was the only thing that was going to make the pain go away (Dr. Bill, right?). He replied, "It hurts too bad to put any weight on it."

Cousin Art Ranta

"Here, I will help you," I said. I helped him up and said, "Put your arm around my neck and I will walk you around the track. You have to walk this off."

This is a very clear memory in my mind. Art would scream when he tried to put weight on the leg, but I assured him that he had to put weight on it even if it hurt because that was the only way he was going to be able to walk it off.

So here we are walking around the track with me helping to hold Art up, with him screaming, while I kept assuring him this is what he needed to do. To make a long story short, I saw Art the next day, and he had a cast on his leg. So naturally I asked him what the doctor had said. "He told me it was broken, and the worst thing I could have done was to walk on it."

I need a broader vocabulary to express, in words, how bad I felt. I don't know if Art noticed how dejected I looked, but I just stood there not knowing what to say. I think he sensed that and came out with a joke: "I hope you don't ever become a doctor; they would probably run you out of

Cousin Wesley Ranta and Bill

town." He laughed and it helped me so much to know that he didn't hold it against me. We were really good friends, and I shall never forget him.

Let me back up to December 1955 when Art and I were in the eighth grade. We decided to go into the woods and cut Christmas trees to sell in town in order to make some spending money. This was no easy task. There was a heavily wooded area at the end of our road where you would turn left to go toward Hautala's corner. All we had was a crosscut saw and an axe. No power saw.

I don't think anyone knew who the property belonged to, and I don't even know if we thought about it. The snow was pretty deep and it was not easy to get around, but here we went. Christmas trees don't grow in the woods for the purpose of being Christmas trees, so it is very unusual to find a tree that was small enough to fit into a house and look uniform.

What we wound up doing was cutting down big trees and then cutting the top off for a Christmas tree. We worked at this project over a couple of weekends. All we had was a two-man crosscut saw for cutting and an axe for trimming. It was hard work. We were huffing and puffing and sometimes we had to stop and rest when we were cutting down a big tree. Then we had to drag them out to the road.

We talked Aunt Jenny, Art's mom, into coming by, and we loaded them on her car. She took them to town and sold them and just held back enough of the money to cover the cost of gas. I don't know how many Christmas trees we were able to stack on her car, but I know she made quite a few trips over the period of two weekends.

When we finished, we left the remains of the big trees lying on the ground (what else could we have done?) and walked off. To this day, I wonder why nobody ever told us that we couldn't cut trees on somebody's property and just walk off and leave a mess. But that is what we did. Hmmm!

My home life became harder and harder to deal with as time went on. Our outhouse was not constructed very well. There were cracks in the walls, and snow would blow through the cracks. Sometimes there would be several inches of snow covering the seat. Can you imagine walking to the outhouse when it is covered with snow and twenty degrees below zero?

Not having running water was another major problem. We had to get the water from a well, and it was so deep that it took a lot of pumping to get the water to the surface. And this had to be done no matter what the weather was like. Washing clothes was a major ordeal. It usually took all weekend. We would have to draw the water from the well, heat it on the wood cook stove, and then wash the clothes by hand using a scrub board inside a washtub.

Then there was the drying process. We tied several ropes across the living room and even one in the kitchen on which to hang the clothes. It was like living in the camp at Wakefield, except we did have electric lights. Keeping the two wood-burning stoves going in the winter was a major problem. I mean major.

Since Dad never made wood ahead of time, splitting wood was a never-ending job. It was especially tough when it had knots in it. Later on, when John was unable to work, different people would deliver wood to us. But for the most part, it didn't help my workload because I had to haul the wood from the road in the winter and split it just like before.

The absolute hardest thing to deal with was the problem of kindling, which was dry wood for starting a fire — mostly cedar. There is no way to start a fire with green hardwood without using kindling first. There just is no way.

We hardly ever had kindling. Sometimes Dad would bring some cedar home, but the majority of the time we did not have any — period! I would often come home from school and have to start a fire in the cook stove, but there would be no kindling. So, I got the bright idea to go behind the blacksmith shed and pull some boards off of the walls and use them for kindling. This worked great as they were really dry.

After I had pulled almost all the boards off the back of that shed, I knew I was going to be in trouble if Dad ever walked back there and saw what I had done. He did eventually find out, slapped me around a bit, and wanted to know why I did it. I told him that there was no kindling, and I didn't know what to do. Can you guess what his response was? "Why didn't you go in the woods and get some little sticks and branches to start the fire?" I just kept quiet as he ranted on. He had been a sergeant in World War II and hollering — loudly — was part of what he was used to doing.

One night while Russell and I were at the milk house listening to a Detroit Tigers baseball game, his mother, Marian, came in and handed me a bottle of milk. She said, "This is for you. Take it home for the family."

Kind, loving neighbor
Marian Saari

When she handed it to me, I noticed a tear coming down her cheek. Dear reader, the ultimate expression of compassion, in my opinion, is when a person sheds tears on behalf of someone else. This is the third time I am relating a tearful gift to me from someone who was not a member of my family. In every incident, it put that person at the top of the list of people who I remembered and cared about the most.

 Marian was a wonderful person and gave us milk many times after that. I will always remember and love her for that. Once when I was sent to the principal's office for fighting, I was sitting in the office waiting to talk to the principal. Marian, who was working in the office, came over to talk to me and asked me why I was there. After I told her, she spoke in such a kind and loving tone that she made it very clear to me that she cared about me. She explained that everything was going to be all right and I needed to remember to be kinder to people. She spoke to me as a mother would, and it really got my attention. I was never again sent to the principal's office because of fighting. For other things, yes, but not for fighting. I will never forget Marian Saari.

L — R: Vice-president, Bill Spetz; President, John Nicksich;
Secretary, Dianne Kapetz; Treasurer, Laverne Niemi

We were in the ninth grade at Roosevelt, and we were the upper classmen. This carried a bit of pride with it as we were now the top dogs in the school. This was a first for me. I had been at Roosevelt longer than I had been at any other school, and it was comforting to know that I was among a class of kids who would graduate together. I felt a close bond with these kids since we had spent three years together. They were my extended family, and I had never felt this close to a group of kids before.

Barbara was nine years old and was helping some around the house. Johnny was seven, but was not really able to help much. Johnny loved the mean roosters and had them all named. When we killed one, we made sure Johnny didn't know about it, especially when we were eating it. It didn't take long for him to realize that one of his roosters was gone. When he asked me if I knew where the rooster was, I did not have the heart to tell him that we ate one of his pet roosters. So, I told him I am pretty sure it ran away. He never did put two and two together.

Dear Johnny, I am sorry I lied to you. I knew better. Please forgive me. So now that you are in your late sixties, I think you can handle the truth. We ate the rooster that I told you ran away. I truly am sorry. Your brother, Bill.

We graduated from Roosevelt with a degree of sadness. I did not look forward to going to Luther L. Wright in Ironwood, where we would not know most of the students. I felt like I was moving from a home environment never to return. Graduating from Roosevelt Junior High ended a period in my life that is, and always will be, the most memorable period in my childhood.

I was now fifteen years old and had started noticing the girls. There were several at Roosevelt who I really liked, but I was handicapped as far as doing anything about it was concerned. I had been driving since I was thirteen years old, but only to run errands. I was not allowed to take the car and go out on a date or visit friends.

I never had a driver's license, but that did not seem to matter very much back in the 1950s. Times were difficult at home and I never had any money of my own. I was allowed to go out on Friday nights, unless I was being punished for something. I did not have any nice clothes to wear, and that always bothered me.

Most of the time, but not always, Dad would manage to come up with fifty cents and give it to me to spend. The problem was that I had to walk and it was a very long walk from our house to downtown Ironwood. Sometimes if Dad had to go to town, he would drop me off. That was not very often. I would stick out my thumb to hitch a ride when a car passed, but not many cars went by, and I rarely got a ride. I would always head for town where the kids would congregate on the corner near the Ironwood Theatre.

One Friday night there was a movie that I was hoping to see playing at the Ironwood Theatre, and I had just enough money to get in. While I was standing in line, I noticed a girl from town who I had seen several times and talked to a few times on our Friday night congregations at the corner.

I finally got up enough nerve to ask her if she would like to sit with me since I was by myself.

She said, "Sure!"

She came over and stood with me in line, and I became a little nervous as I was thinking, *Is this a date? And if it is, isn't it my responsibility to pay her way into the movie?* I sure hoped not because I did not have enough money to pay for both of us. My fears were put to rest when she stepped up and paid her own way into the movie.

I had gone to a lot of movies in my young life but had never sat next to a girl who wasn't family. We chatted a little, but it was mostly her doing the talking. I was very shy around girls.

Then she came up with a request that made me sink into my seat: "I sure would like some popcorn, wouldn't you?"

This was a killer. I had to admit something that I would have rather taken a beating than to admit, as I replied to her, "I would, but I do not have any money."

She very cordially said, "I think I have enough," as she started counting her change. She did have enough money, and she jumped up and said, "I will be right back."

It seemed like she was gone forever as I sat there thinking. *There is no way she is going to like me. I am not dressed nice, I do not have a car to drive, and now she knows that I do not have any money either.*

She came back with the popcorn and we sat there and shared it as the movie was playing. I really didn't want any by this time, but I did nibble on a few kernels. It took me half the movie to get up enough nerve to put my arm around her neck. When I did, she tilted her head slightly and laid her head on my shoulder. *Now what? Where do we go from here? She must like me a little or she wouldn't have laid her head on my shoulder.*

When the movie was over and we had walked outside, I felt like I had no choice other than to tell her good-bye. I knew I couldn't buy her a coke or a shake or anything, so we said good-bye. And that was it.

This one incident contributed greatly to my low self-esteem at this point in my life. I not only was very unhappy, but I had no way or means of pursuing happiness. The heavy depression sets in when you are in a very unhappy circumstance without being able to see any way out. I was not in control and had no other choice but to accept things the way they were.

Dear reader, don't let anyone tell you there is nothing wrong with being poor. I can tell you from personal experience that there is plenty wrong with being poor. I hated it. If everyone was as poor as I was, I would have been fine, but the problem was that I was the poorest kid I knew. I lived in snow country and never owned a sled, or skis, or ice skates. I never owned a bicycle or a basketball or a football, either. I could not go anywhere with any of my friends to do things because I did not have the equipment necessary to do them.

The movie incident had me thinking, for the first time, about running away. The Roosevelt years were behind me and I was going to embark on a new chapter in my life. Again, this was not by choice but necessity.

13

On to Luther L. Wright

I THINK A CERTAIN SADNESS showed in my face when I attended Roosevelt Junior High. I rarely smiled and there was a caption under my picture in the 1957 yearbook that read: *He is sober as a judge, but he likes a good time.*

I was a little apprehensive when it was time to start my sophomore year at Luther L. Wright for the 1957-58 school year. I was fifteen and would turn sixteen before the school year ended. I suppose most kids would be happy to start high school because it

Luther L. Wright High School
(now grades K-12)

was a big step up the elevator of life, and certain dreams and aspirations were bound to be swirling in their heads. For me, it was not easy to be happy about anything while carrying this very heavy burden of low self-esteem.

The thought of meeting all these new kids in a setting that I did not know also worried me. Changing schools was something I really didn't want. Roosevelt was a country school located in Ironwood

Township. Luther L. Wright was the high school in the City of Ironwood. At that time, it also housed Gogebic Junior College on the third floor. There would be about sixty of us making this transition, and we would comprise only twenty-five percent of the sophomore class. The rest of the kids were from town.

The bus no longer came to our driveway. Now we had to walk about a mile to the bus stop. There were many mornings in the winter when we stood waiting for the bus that we could hardly wait for it to come because we were so cold. We knew the bus had heat. It felt so good to go up those few bus steps and sit in a heated environment. It was not uncommon to go to school in the winter when it was twenty degrees below zero, and sometimes colder.

Fortunately, I had matured a little by now and realized that lashing out at people and fighting would definitely not be appropriate, so I kept a low profile.

I did love basketball and tried out for the basketball team that year. A lot of kids were trying out and it was obvious not all would make the team. Coach Betchek told us a list would be posted on the bulletin board the next day by lunch time. It would have the names of those who made the team.

As soon as we broke for lunch, I hurried to the bulletin board and there it was — my name! Wow! I would be playing for the Ironwood Red Devils on the high school basketball team. How about that? I couldn't have been happier. I had attended football and basketball games when I was in grade school in Ironwood, and now I would be playing for them. It was like I had made the major league.

I was placed on the B team, but that was not really a disappointment because I was new to the school and there were already established starters. I was certain that I would move up to the varsity team after practicing hard and showing them what I could do.

One major obstacle that had not even crossed my mind caused this dream to crash. Basketball practice was after school, and I had no transportation or anyone willing to pick me up and bring me home. At first my resolve was strong, and I would start out walking and hitchhiking. Sometimes I would get a ride part way, but never the full distance. Other times I had to walk all the way.

This became more and more difficult as it got colder. I remember arriving home so numb that I thought my hands and fingers were going to fall off. I didn't have the warm clothing required to endure the bitter cold and snow. In addition to that, Dad had reached the point where he was unable to work.

It was hard for Dad to get a fire going in the cook stove and put the potatoes on. Sometimes when he had managed to start the fire and get the potatoes on while I was away, there would be no wood in the house. I would have to go outside, split it, and bring it in.

I would get ahead of the game by splitting wood on weekends and bringing it in, but the wood ran out before the week was over, and I had to start the whole process again. Dad finally told me that he couldn't handle doing it anymore. Rheumatoid arthritis had set in to the point that he could hardly move. He told me that I would have to quit basketball.

I was already thinking along those lines when he told me, but it still caused a wave of depression to come over me. I didn't blame him. I just felt like a failure and this added more to the load of low self-esteem that I was already carrying.

I was so down that I didn't handle the situation well. I should have gone to Coach Betchek or Coach Ostrom to explain my situation and tell them why I had to quit. Instead, I stopped showing up for practice. Now I felt like I was not only a quitter but also a coward for not facing the problem.

The following year, my junior year, I had a plan. I would go out for basketball again and if I made the team — and there was no doubt that I would — I would talk to everybody I knew in the family and see if I could get someone to give me a ride home from practice. I would even talk to Coach Betchek and Coach Ostrom to see if they could help me.

Coaches Betchek and Ostrom

The same scenario as the year before transpired, but when I went to see the bulletin board at lunch — lo and behold — my name was not on it. I couldn't believe it. *How could I not make the team if I made it as a sophomore?* Now I was a junior, better than I was the year before. I had grown at least another inch and had played a lot of intramural basketball during lunch and at the Resettlement. Coach Torro had even told me that he could see my improvement.

It bothered me to the point that I went to Coach Betchek to talk to him about it. He explained that the reason my name was not on the list was that I had quit the year before and never said a word to anybody, and there was no room on the team for quitters.

Despite my total despair, I knew his reasoning was just. It was over. The dream of playing basketball for the Ironwood Red Devils was over, and I could only blame myself.

Ray was no longer a part of my life. He had just taken off for Chicago to live with Dolly and Frank, who was one of three partners in a heating business that dealt with large furnaces. The name of their business was Beverly Heating. He and Frank really hit it off. Ray was a good worker and Frank put him to work. The thought just occurred to me — they were both Polish! Hmmm! I wonder if that had something to do with it?

Frank and Dolly had moved to a suburb of Chicago called Blue Island. They had built an upstairs apartment over the company shop, and it was nice. I did see it a year or two later and was very impressed with how nice it was.

Mrs. Farrow's Homeroom 104
Bill is in the back row, third from left

It was almost impossible to make new friends at Luther L. Wright because the only place I would see classmates was in class. Because of my home situation, I was never able to attend any after school activities and because I lived so far from town, I was unable to hang out with them after school or on weekends. My friends from Roosevelt were all scattered because of the larger school and so many more classrooms.

I continued to go to town on Friday nights. I would get together with a few of my friends, and we would pool our money and have someone go to a store and buy beer for us. I remember we used to get Edelweiss beer really cheap, but it was not refrigerated. Then we would go to the cemetery, chug-a-lug the beer, and head for town with a major buzz going. Sometimes we would go to Bruce Crossing and drink because they were not strict on asking for IDs. This drinking only happened when I would manage to come up with a couple of bucks, or when one of the other kids had money and was willing to share.

This was the extent of my social life during my Luther L. Wright years. Life was basically get up and get the fire going in both stoves, get ready for school with no running water, take the bus to school, come home and get the fires going again, put the potatoes on, eat supper, clean off the table, heat water to do the dishes, listen to music on the radio, sit around, and then go to bed. We never had a phone the whole time we lived at the old George Koski home.

There were a few girls I really liked, but it was impossible to pursue a relationship with a girl if you had no money, no car to use, and no way to even call them. Asking a girl for a date was simply out of the question.

During this time, Barbara lived with different people for short periods of time. For instance, she would spend a couple of weeks with Aunt Mary Niemi and sometimes with other people who I can't recall. It seems like people have a tendency to feel more compassion for a little girl without a mother than they do for a couple of mean little boys.

Several years later, Barbara moved into the Bigford household. Dr. Bigford was a dentist and his wife, Bert, and Barbara became very close friends for a number of years. They had several small children and Barbara would help out with them. They would buy Barbara nice clothes and later helped her go to a private college.

Some years after that, Barbara married a man from Atlanta, Georgia, who became a dentist. They ended up doing dental work on an Indian reservation in Arizona. Barbara had many exciting stories to tell about her life on the reservation. Later, they moved to Atlanta, where her husband David was from, and opened a private practice.

At this time, Dad was in a tremendous amount of pain and was taking a lot of medication. Fortunately, he was still able to drive and get around well enough that he could go to the doctor's office. Even though I would drive to run errands, for some reason he never asked me to take him to the doctor. He had also started using a cane.

It was time to enter Luther L. Wright for the 1958-59 school year. This was my junior year, and just like before, I was not thrilled about going. The routine was pretty much the same as the previous year. We would catch the bus and get off at Ed's Campus Kitchen, which was just across the street from the high school. Our bus driver dropped us off an hour before school started because he had another route to run.

Bill at the Gogebic
County Fair

My brother, Ray, was in Blue Island, Illinois, working for Frank and I really missed him. Barbara was living with different people, so I didn't see much of her either. Johnny, on the other hand, was always here. So, it was Dad, Johnny, and me who were the only ones at home.

One day, early in the winter of 1958, we were all hanging out at Ed's Campus Kitchen waiting for school to start when out of nowhere my brother Ray walked in. I couldn't believe it. I hadn't seen him in well over a year, and there he was. I was so excited that I couldn't help giving him a big hug. He had decided to come home for a visit.

The first thing he said to me was, "Just forget about going to school today. We are going shopping." That sounded great to me. I wasn't even worried about getting in trouble for missing school. I was going to spend the day with my brother.

When Ray left Blue Island, he obviously had just been paid, and maybe he had also been saving his money. He had a pocketful, the best that I could tell. "The first thing we are going to do is buy you a good warm coat," he said. "Then we are going to buy you some nice clothes."

Talk about being excited; I was more than that. First, I would be with my brother, and second, I would be getting some new clothes. I didn't have many clothes, just a few pairs of badly worn pants and maybe three or four shirts that were threadbare.

What a day! We went all over town shopping. He bought me a really nice winter coat, five new shirts (he wanted me to have a new one for each day of the school week), three or four pairs of pants, socks, underwear, shoes, and warm winter boots. I was in my glory. I changed at one of the stores and put on my new shirt, pants, socks, shoes, and coat. I threw everything away that I had taken off. I couldn't remember the last time I had new clothes.

We ate breakfast in town, and later we had lunch. We had bags of stuff we were hauling around, and finally we decided to go back to school and catch the bus home. The driver let Ray ride with us.

Ray stayed only a few days, and then he was gone again. He joined the Marines and wound up in California for his basic training. I never understood how he pulled off this enlistment because he would not be eighteen until October, but he did it. Maybe they let younger guys in the military back then — I don't know.

Brother Ray and his family living in Broadview, 1969

So, Ray was gone again. We never lived together after that, but I will always treasure those few days we spent together in 1958.

I had started smoking at the age of thirteen and did a good job of hiding my habit from Dad. Cigarettes were hard to come by without much money to buy them. Now that I was in high school, it was easier to find kids who had cigarettes and were willing to share them with me. Smoking was not frowned on, like it is now. In fact, we were allowed to smoke on the school bus on the way to school. The only stipulations were that we had to sit in the back of the bus and make sure that we picked up all of our cigarette butts when we exited.

Ed's was the perfect teen hangout. Ed would let us smoke, and smoke we would. He had a jukebox that was kept cranking the whole time we were there. He also had pinball machines that were very popular during this time. Most of us would gather around the pinball machines, and if we weren't playing, we would watch whoever was playing.

I shall never forget this day as long as I live — Wednesday, February 4, 1959. This was a period in my life when I was into the new rock music of the day that Elvis had started three or four years before. There was a buzz going around the school about a rock and roll concert coming up in Moorhead, Minnesota, approximately three hundred fifty miles straight west from Ironwood on the western border of Minnesota. It seemed far away, but it was an easy drive (weather permitting), about six and a half or seven hours.

I really wanted to go, and a friend of mine, Jack Engberg, and I talked about it, wishing we could go, but we were well aware of the fact that we did not have the money and were just dreaming. However, a group from our school was going, and we were a little jealous of them.

So, here I am on this day, playing the pinball machine at Ed's, prior to the start of school. In walked Jack and he came straight over to me with a very solemn look on his face. "We don't have to feel bad about not going to the concert," he said.

"Why?" I asked.

"They're all dead."

"Who are you talking about?"

"Buddy Holly, The Big Bopper, and Ritchie Valens," he explained.

I was stunned. This couldn't be. Ironically, one of my favorite songs was "La Bamba" by Ritchie Valens, and it was playing on the jukebox while we were having this discussion.

I just turned away from the pinball machine and told the kid next to me that he could finish my game if he cared to. I wanted to talk with Jack.

The first thing I wanted to know was when this had happened and how he knew about it. "It happened yesterday. I heard about it when I got home from school last night. They were in a small plane and had left Clear Lake, Iowa, headed to Moorhead, and their plane crashed," he murmured.

I was reeling. I loved their music and thought they were all great. I had memorized a lot of their music and sang most of their songs when I was at home by myself. I was really having a hard time digesting this. News traveled slowly back then. We did not have a television at our house, only a small radio. But all I ever listened to was music. I was not interested in the news at this point in my life. We did get a daily paper, but because of where we lived, we got it a day late.

Now that I am in the latter years of my life, I realize how much music influences us. This one incident, about sixty years ago, had such a profound effect on me that it is burned into my memory bank, and will probably be there until the day that I no longer will be involved in this life.

To a lot of us who lived back then and even some who came along a lot later, Don McLean put it best in his song "American Pie," when he referred to this very dramatic incident as "The Day the Music Died."

It seemed like everything in my life was falling apart, and I was getting to the point where I was having a hard time handling it. I wanted to be able to do something about my situation. I felt helpless. I started thinking seriously about running away and getting a job, perhaps my own car, and being able to live a normal life.

This was going to be the hardest decision I would ever have to make at this point in my life. Mother was gone, Dolly was gone, Aunt Betty was gone, Ray was gone, Barbara was gone, and I couldn't see my brother, Ronnie. I was totally broke, and felt unloved. There was no way to even think about having fun.

I really think at this point in my life, I was a good candidate for a nervous breakdown. I was totally depressed and unhappy. I reasoned that Johnny was close to ten years old and was old enough to help Dad around the house. I felt that if I left, there would be one less mouth to feed. I decided to go for it, but I did not feel good about my decision. I worried about Dad and Johnny and how they would manage with me gone.

My plan was to hitchhike to Chicago and stay with my father long enough to get a job and my own place. I never contacted my father because I thought I might change my mind before I got there. This was scary, but I felt I could not continue living the way I was. Yes, the pain of staying was worse than the pain of leaving.

Sometime in early March of 1959, I made the decision to leave. I was sixteen years old and would be seventeen in a couple of months. I got up that particular morning and rode the school bus to school. But instead of going into Ed's, which was my norm, I began walking toward downtown Ironwood and into Hurley. My plan was to start hitchhiking at the corner of Hwy. 51 and Silver Street in Hurley. I was a little nervous, but had built up a little stronger resolve.

I had managed to come up with seventy-five cents by saving every penny I could get my hands on for several weeks. I knew this would be enough to get something to eat and tide me over until I got to Chicago. I was running away from home. I was determined, but not happy about it.

Leaving Roosevelt, 1957

14
Running Away

IT WAS A COLD DAY in March of 1959 when I began hitchhiking from Hurley, Wisconsin, headed for Chicago. Fortunately, I had a warm coat and all new clothes, thanks to my brother Ray. I did not pack anything, so I only had the clothes I was wearing. This was a bit of a bummer because Ray had bought me some nice clothes, and I had to leave them behind. Dad was up the morning I left, and I knew it would arouse suspicion if I started packing clothes.

I still hadn't called Father to tell him I was coming to stay with him. I wasn't totally sure I wouldn't change my mind and turn around and head back home. I was relatively sure he would not turn me away and would help me get on my feet.

Hitchhiking was a good way for someone without money to get around back then. It was not hard to get a ride because people traveling alone seemed to like the company of another person. It was not considered as dangerous as it is now. There never was a doubt in my mind that people would not stop to pick me up, and I wasn't concerned about getting a ride. My only concern was how many rides it would take and how long I would be on the road.

I got a few short rides from people who were going to the next town, and I finally wound up near Wausau, Wisconsin, where I was picked up by a truck driver named Chuck Goldsmith. This turned out to be the best thing that could have possibly happened to me on this trip.

Chuck informed me that he was also a professional wrestler. I thought that was so cool. He gave me one of his business cards with a picture of him in the ring getting ready to wrestle. I kept it for several years before I ended up losing it. He told me he was from Milwaukee and had a few stops to make before heading for home. He then asked if I wanted to ride with him and spend the night at his house. In the morning, since he was not going to Chicago, he would drop me off at an intersection where I could get a ride to Chicago. That sounded fine with me. We stopped at a truck stop and he bought me something to eat. I really enjoyed eating a good meal and I appreciated him buying it for me. I was now down to twenty-five cents, and I knew that wouldn't buy much.

When we finally got to Milwaukee it was getting late. We pulled into this big trucking company's parking lot where he left his truck, and we got into his car and headed to his home. I am not sure where in Milwaukee we were headed, but I remember he lived with his wife in an upstairs apartment in some business district.

It was pretty late when we finally arrived at his apartment. When we got inside it was dark, and as he turned on the light, he called out to his wife, "Honey, I'm home and we have company."

I assume she had been in bed because she came into the living room wearing a robe and looking kind of sleepy. She glanced at me and then looked at Chuck and said, "And who is this?"

I immediately felt uncomfortable. Here I was in a strange environment with a man who I had just met and a woman who I had never met. Chuck introduced me as Bill and told her about picking me up and that I needed a place to sleep because I would be leaving early in the morning. She seemed to brighten up a bit as she welcomed me to their home and took me to the bedroom where I would be sleeping. She was super nice, and I started feeling at ease as she showed me the bathroom and the location of the towels and washcloths. She then excused herself and said she was going back to bed because she had to work in the morning. Chuck and I stayed up and talked awhile before we went to bed.

It was hard to fall asleep when I finally laid down. There were a lot of things going through my mind as I wondered what Dad and Johnny were going to say or do when they discovered I wasn't there. This thought choked me up a little, and I had to keep telling myself that this would end up being good for everyone in the long run. As time went by, Dad had started receiving his disability check and they were able to move to a much nicer house in Ironwood Township. This house even had running water and a commode. It also had a sauna about twenty yards from the house. I went back many times as I got older and there was no doubt that Johnny would enjoy a better lifestyle than I had at his age. This made me extremely happy.

I woke up the next morning as daylight was breaking. As I headed to the bathroom, I could hear Chuck and his wife talking in the kitchen. I went back to my room and looked out the window and realized that we were indeed in a business district in an upstairs apartment, probably above a store because there were stores everywhere. This was not a main street since it was too narrow for that, but it was in the business district for sure

I thought, *Yesterday morning I was getting up in Ironwood Township walking to catch the bus, and here I am approximately twenty-four hours later in Milwaukee, Wisconsin, wondering what is going to happen next.*

I heard Chuck say good-bye to his wife and heard the door close. It wasn't long after when Chuck knocked on my door to see if I was awake. When I told him I was, he said his wife had fixed me some breakfast, and after I ate, we would have to get going.

I was ready to start the day. It was like this was the first day of my freedom, and at this point I was in control of whatever I wanted to do. I was excited as I sat down to eat breakfast. This was a real treat for me. It had been years since anyone had fixed me breakfast, and it made me feel special. What a nice lady! I guess Chuck had already eaten because he sat across from me at the table drinking coffee as we talked.

We left the apartment and drove back to the trucking company so Chuck could pick up his truck. I noticed that when we left the apartment, he had a shopping bag in his hand, and I wondered what was in it. As we drove to the intersection where he was going to drop me off, he asked me to pull out the wrestling card that he had given me the night before as he handed me a pen. He asked me to write down his address and phone number on the back of the card and keep it with me. He then told me that if things didn't work out in Chicago to just give him a call and he would see what he could do to help me find a job. I could also stay with them until I was financially able to be on my own.

I cannot find the words to express how happy that made me feel. I was blown away at how kind he and his wife had been. This offer meant a lot because it was like a security blanket. I had someone to fall back on if I needed help, and that had me pumped up as he stopped the truck to let me out.

When I started to open the door, he said, "Hey Bill, here is a little sack lunch that my wife made for you." He reached into the shopping bag and pulled out a bag with a sandwich, an apple, and a candy bar in it and handed it to me. Then he said, "Here is something else for you." He reached into his shirt pocket, pulled out a $5 bill, and handed it to me.

Wow! I felt like I was rich. I wanted to give him a big hug but I thought better of it. He was this macho wrestling guy and giving him a hug just didn't seem appropriate. So, I shook his hand and thanked him for everything he had done for me.

I felt sad as I watched him drive away. His kindness toward me has stayed with me for all these years. When I finally got settled in Chicago, I wrote Chuck a long letter thanking him for everything and told him that if things didn't work out, I would call him.

As the years rolled by, I often wondered why he took such a liking to me. I thought perhaps he had seen some of his childhood memories in me. It was possible we had similar childhoods. He did mention that he had been on his own since he was sixteen years old, and he knew I was now officially on my own at that same age. Thank you, Chuck, for helping me along the highway of life. I shall never forget you.

I was not sure where we were when he dropped me off, but it was a very busy intersection. He pointed and said, "That is the way to Chicago — just stand there and stick out your thumb." I felt pretty alone at this point. I was not used to all this traffic and it made me a bit nervous. I did, however, realize I was not in bad shape. I had some food and five dollars in my pocket. What a great guy! I was in much better shape than when I had left Ironwood.

Dear reader, five dollars was a lot of money in 1959. I could not ever remember having that much money since we worked making hay. This money equated to ten hours of making hay.

I didn't have to stand there very long before a man stopped and picked me up. He asked me where I was going. And when I told him I was going to Chicago, he told me I was in luck because he was headed for the Loop in downtown Chicago. This was great. I had already planned that wherever I wound up, I would call my father and ask him if he would come and pick me up.

When I got out of the car, I was in a crowd of bustling people in downtown Chicago. Now I needed to find a phone booth to call my father, but I was not sure how to do that. It was then that I spotted a really fancy-looking hotel, and I reasoned that if I went in there that they would surely have phones. I approached the desk and asked the desk clerk if they had a phone that I could use. He pointed over to the corner of the lobby where there were about four phone booths linked together. This was truly my lucky day.

I had my father's phone number written on a scrap of paper folded up in the billfold that Ray had bought me, and I had change in my pocket to use the phone. I called my father on his home phone and he answered almost immediately. Fortunately, this was a Saturday, or my father would have been at work and unable to answer the phone. I told Father where I was and asked him if he would come and get me. He seemed excited and said he would leave immediately. I told him the name of the hotel and said I would wait in the lobby.

This was a huge lobby and I had no trouble finding somewhere to sit. I don't remember ever sitting on furniture that was so plush and comfortable. This was uptown Chicago and I knew I was in the high-rent district. I just hoped no one would come over to me and ask me to leave, as it was apparent that I was not a guest there. Nobody ever did.

I sat in a position so that I could see the front door. It didn't seem like a very long time before I saw my father walk in. I stood up and waved as I approached him. He was all smiles as he gave me a big hug and said how happy he was to see me.

I never loved my father like a son should love his father. I have some guilt feelings about that, especially as I get older. It was not his fault that our home was broken. The fault lay at the feet of my mother, since she left him for another man.

This is where I need to stop and say that a child does not necessarily deal in logic. Children deal mostly in feelings. I loved my mother supremely no matter what she had done. I held it against my father for taking me away from my mother in the early custody hearings, and attempting unsuccessfully to take me away from Dad, Dolly, Barbara, and Johnny in the custody hearing after Mother had passed away. Through it all, I did have enough respect for my father that I was always courteous to him when we spoke, and I did hide the resentment I felt toward him as best as I could.

The ride from downtown Chicago to Broadview was fairly nice. The first person I asked about was Al. I was surprised to find out that Al and Coral were married and had a daughter named Bethel. I also asked about Chuck Lawrence and the other neighborhood kids. Chuck and his family, who were living next door when I last lived there in 1954, had moved to Westchester, another suburb of Chicago a few miles away. It sounded like all the neighborhood kids were still around — only five years older. Father and Marie had moved to the basement and I would be staying in one of the basement rooms and that was fine with me. We did have a commode, but not a bathtub. I would go upstairs every Friday and take a bath at Al and Coral's apartment.

Now, I was ready to embark on a new chapter in my life. Here I was sixteen years old, soon to be seventeen, and I had been on an emotional roller coaster my whole life.

It started with my mother divorcing my father, and soon after that, there was a custody battle in which Father was awarded custody of me. Then Mother kidnapped me and moved all of us to Florida. Next my mother passed away and there was another custody battle. I lost my brother Ronnie; my sister Dolly left, and then Aunt Betty. I had been kidnapped once and ran away from home twice, and I had been raised in total poverty. The final blow was Ray leaving to be on his own. Through it all, I managed to survive and was up for my new challenge.

So here I was back in Broadview, Illinois, and I desperately wanted to get a job and have my own money. My father wanted me to finish high school, but I was adamant about going to work. He tried his best to talk me into going back to school. I understood that he wanted me to get an education, but I did not want to go to school and be a kid who was broke. I was tired of being a kid. I wanted to have my own money and was more than willing to work for it.

Father finally consented and helped me to get a job at the same place he worked. I was excited about going to work and earning my own money. The dream I had of having my own place to live and having my own car to drive was totally dependent on getting a job and going to work. I was ready to embark on my work career, and was excited and a little nervous.

Since I had already spent two summers living there before, I knew several of the neighborhood kids. We were all teenagers now, but picked back up with the friendships we had formed approximately five years earlier. The most notable was Chuck Lawrence, who had now moved a few miles away. Chuck had finished high school and went to work for his father as a painter. His father was a well-established painting contractor in the area and seemed to be successful.

Chuck was probably two years older than I was and had just bought a brand new 1959 Ford Fairlane. It was black with red upholstery. Sharp! He was more than happy to take me anywhere I wanted and he loved to be on the go with that car. He would come over almost every night, and the first thing he would say was, "Where do you want to go?"

I was amazed at this. For the first time in my life I was going somewhere with a friend. We went everywhere together, including Ironwood many times. He even met a girl in Ironwood who he dated for a while. We remained very close friends until he passed away some years ago. I miss him.

I went back to Ironwood countless times in the next year or two. In fact, my first airline flight was to Ironwood. My dad did not seem to hold it against me that I ran away. I would always manage to give him some money to help them out. He was always a little reluctant to take it, but he would finally accept it and thank me profusely. A few years later, I was able to buy Johnny a motor scooter that he used for a long time. I felt good about being able to do that for him. I loved my brother.

I was also able to rekindle my relationship with my "brother" Al, who was Marie's only son. He had married his college sweetheart, Coral, and they had a two-year-old daughter named Bethel. Coral was pregnant again and would have their second daughter, Dawn, shortly after I arrived. Their family rounded out some years later with a total of four girls and one boy. He would take me to

One of many ball games
Bill and Al attended

play volleyball, swimming, and baseball games. Sometimes we would play catch in the yard. He was like another brother to me, and I think of him often.

I started my job at J. W. Johnson and was happy to start receiving a regular paycheck. My father was not entirely happy that I refused to go back to school, so he had the attitude that there was not going to be a free ride here. That was okay with me. I had never had a free ride before and wasn't expecting one now. I didn't have to start fires every day, chop and haul wood, carry water from the well, go to the outhouse to use the bathroom, and wash clothes by hand. We even had hot water. I just had to worry about keeping my room clean.

My father charged me for the room on a weekly basis and also charged me gas money for his car because I was riding to work with him. Marie also charged me to wash my clothes. Actually, I was fine with that. I didn't have to do it myself, and I don't remember it costing me very much money.

I was so happy when I started receiving money every week. I needed a lot of things and knew it would take a while to get them. Marie had taken me shopping a day or so after I got there because I did not have any clothes. She bought me several pairs of pants and some shirts to get by on. We wore uniforms at work. My first priority when I started making money was to buy clothes.

When my mother was alive, she took us to church every week. Many of the things that I had learned about God and the plan of salvation were embedded in my brain, and I prayed a lot. I would consistently pray that the Lord would help me to carry this heavy burden and to keep it from crushing me. He always seemed to give me enough strength to carry on. I also asked Him to bless me in my work, so that I could help others and be a blessing to those who were less fortunate than me.

I would cry out to Him at night sometimes, and I knew He heard me because my life began to change for the better. I was now able to see the light at the end of the tunnel. I was beginning to make friends at work and at home. I was also able to visit my grandmother and quite a few of my Italian relatives on my mother's side of the family.

The guilt that I had from leaving home began to subside as I felt that my dad and Johnny were all right and doing a lot better since I left. Barbara was in a good situation living with Dr. Bigford and his wife, Bert. Barbara helped with the children and helped Dr. Bigford in his dental office in Wakefield. They kept her in nice clothes and sent her to a private academy some years later. I was missing Ray, but that would soon change.

There was still something missing that caused me an inner loneliness. I was about to turn seventeen, and I had never been on a real date. I longed for someone I could have a real relationship with, someone who I could really care about, and who would care about me in return. I knew something would happen that would bring this about, but I wasn't sure just when.

The girl across the street was really cute and we had all played together when we were kids. She was one year older than me and she had blossomed since the last time I saw her. Her parents were quite well off. They owned a beauty shop and they were both hair dressers with several employees. It was 1959, and they had bought her a beautiful 1957 two-tone red and white Chevy convertible. Although it wasn't brand new, it was in immaculate condition. I sure would like to have that car now.

Anyway, she took me for a ride in it and we stopped at an A&W root beer stand and had a root beer. I was not comfortable with her, although she was very pretty and nice. I think I was intimidated because she had a nice car and dressed immaculately — I didn't own a car and my clothes were very, very ordinary. I was old-school even back then when I was young. I did not want to have a relationship with a girl when I didn't have a car and she did. We had many conversations in the street and I really did like her, but I decided not to pursue her.

I had a few house rules that I was expected to live by, but they really weren't very bad at all. I had a curfew on weeknights when we would be working the next day. They didn't want me coming home in the wee hours of the morning and waking them up. Other than that, I could pretty much do whatever I wanted.

Father knew I was pretty independent because of fending for myself for a lot of years, and so he let me go wherever I wanted. It was definitely not like a real father-son relationship. Since I needed to live there until I could afford to live on my own, it was in my best interest to try to get along, which I think I did quite well.

Bill, living in his father's house on Field Avenue

15 My First Date

A LOT OF THINGS HAPPENED in my life in 1959. I had started working in March of that year, and my goal was to live a normal life. Being wealthy was never my goal. I wanted a life where I could make my own decisions and a life that would be well above the poverty level. I had a strong resolve and was willing to put forth the effort to bring this to fruition.

To get my first job was a step toward these goals. I wanted my own place that would have the things that we all take for granted in this day and age. I just thought it would be so cool to have a place where I could take a bath or shower inside of my own apartment or house. I wanted to be able to see the results of the effort that I was getting ready to put out.

The most exciting thing at this point in my life was that I was in charge of my own destiny. The unhappiness I had suffered through my entire childhood was beyond my control. I was a child in an adult world with no power or authority to change any of my circumstances. Now, it would be different, and I hoped and prayed for the best.

I did get to see my sister Dolly quite often since she lived in Blue Island, another suburb of Chicago. It was pretty far south of

Chicago and a long drive. My father would occasionally let me take his car to visit her, but I had to bring the car back that same day. Chuck Lawrence would often take me there, and I would spend the weekend with Dolly. He would then come and get me on Sunday night. These were fun times.

Frank and Dolly now had two children — Diana and Peggy. Some years later they had their only son, Paul. Dolly treated me wonderfully. They were doing fairly well financially and she would take me roller skating and out to eat quite often. Frank would take us all out to eat on Sunday afternoon on many occasions. These were wonderful times.

It wasn't very long after that, perhaps in May or June, that I contacted Ray, who was still in Ironwood. I had turned seventeen in May, and he would be turning eighteen in October. He had married a local girl named Jean Baschand, and she was pregnant with their first child, Teresa, who is now on my friends list on Facebook. Teresa was born later that year. I told Ray that the place where I was working was hiring, and he decided to come to Broadview to see if he could also get a job working at J. W. Johnson Co.

He was familiar with the area just as I was, from when we were there for two summers. Talk about being excited — I really was. Lester and Marie decided to rent the upstairs apartment to them, and they had asked me if I would like to live with them to help share expenses. I would pay one-third of the rent and one-third of the grocery bills. This was a great arrangement from a financial standpoint, and it worked well for a while. Ray got the job, and all three of us would ride together to work.

I loved being around my brother again, but it was not the same. He was newly married and in love, and I felt out of place. I did have my own bedroom, and we had a full bathroom with a tub that I really liked. Since the baby was coming, they would need more room. I decided it would be best for all of us if I found another place to live.

There were a lot of people at our workplace from northern Mississippi, and most of them seemed to know each other. There was a lot of poverty in the area where they were from. I reasoned that some of them had gotten a job here originally, and they told their friends and relatives about it. Thus, a lot of them came to work at J. W. Johnson Co. When I say a lot, I mean a lot of people from

Mississippi worked there, so much so that I felt a little out of place with my Yankee brogue from the UP of Michigan.

They were very nice people and very friendly. One such person was James Key. James and I were close to the same age and hit it off almost immediately when I started working there. He had been staying with family members the same as I was, and he was looking to find a place also. This was great! We could get a furnished apartment and share expenses. So that is exactly what we did. It was in a suburb called Melrose Park and perhaps a little closer to work than when I lived in Broadview, but it was in the opposite direction. Broadview was south of Bellwood, where we worked, and Melrose Park was north.

Now we had another obstacle to overcome. We had no transportation. Another man worked with us named Jimmy McWherter. James knew him from back home in Boonville, Mississippi, where they had once lived close to each other. Jimmy had a car and lived in Melrose Park also, so we offered him money to pick us up and bring us home. He readily agreed to that.

James and I had been talking about buying a car together. We had it all planned out. He would have total control over the car to do whatever he wanted for one week, and then it would be my turn to control the car for one week and go wherever I wanted. We would swap each week.

Do you see anything bad coming? Caution: Do not go partners on buying a car unless you are married. Never! *Period!*

Our other obstacle was that neither one of us had credit. I was seventeen and he was eighteen. Enter Jimmy McWherter. How we pulled this off, I do not know, but we talked Jimmy into cosigning for us.

Double caution: Do not ever cosign for anyone. *Ever!*

So, we bought this 1955 black Ford that had been a police car. In fact, it had dual spotlights, and we both liked it a lot.

I was thrilled that I now had access to a car, even if it was every other week. We both looked forward to weekends because through the week we had to ride to and from work. Not so on weekends.

Problems started almost immediately. Jimmy had a girlfriend in Mississippi, and when it was his turn to have the car, he would get off work and head to Mississippi for the weekend. He would usually get back late Sunday night. A few times he stayed an extra day and just called in sick. This created a problem for me because I would have to find someone to take me to work on Monday. Here he was piling the miles on the car since it was around 1,200 miles round trip from where we lived to Boonville, Mississippi. There wasn't much I could say or do about it. I had the right to do the same thing, but for the most part, I didn't.

This rocked along for about two or three months, and then *blam!* James left on Friday, as he usually did, and never came back. Ever! I got the word through the Mississippi grapevine that he had totaled the car in an accident and did not want to come back and face the music. There was no insurance on the car.

This is where my immaturity kicked in. Jimmy McWherter was on the hook to pay for the car now, and he came to me for help, which is as it should be. However, in my young mind, I figured James had wrecked it so he should have to pay for it.

I refused. Now Jimmy was really angry. He didn't wreck the car, but he had to pay for it. Later in life, when I finally figured out that I was in the wrong, I tried to look him up and give his money back, but I never could find him. The people in Mississippi had heard he moved to Arkansas, but nobody knew where. When I first got my computer, I tried looking him up, but to no avail. I still feel bad about that situation. Here was a guy nice enough to help us get a car, and we ended up sticking him with paying for it.

I was back to square one. I could pay the rent myself, but barely. Also, I no longer had a car. This is now going through my mind: *What does it take to get ahead? And what will I have to do to get a car?* My father refused to cosign, and I can't say that I blamed him. I didn't have much choice. I moved back into the basement with my father and Marie and rode with Father and Ray to work, just like before. By now, we were approaching the end of the year as we celebrated Ray's eighteenth birthday on October 20, 1959.

Sometime in November of 1959 I noticed this cute girl from Mississippi who had just come to work at J. W. Johnson Co. Her name was Edna Mock, and her sister and brother-in-law were already working there. I had gotten to know her sister, Betty Sue, and her husband, James. Betty Sue told me all about her sister, Edna, and that she would be coming there to work. She told me Edna was single and had just ended a bad relationship with her boyfriend who, by the way, ended up being a judge in Tishomingo County where she was a resident.

I kind of watched her for about a week and noticed she was very shy, but a good worker. Then I noticed when we went on break that she would always sit close to where I sat. *Hmmm! Maybe she likes me.* I wasn't sure, but I decided to ask her if she would like to go to a drive-in movie sometime. Since I didn't have a car, I figured it would be smart on my part to find out if she would go out with

Edna, early 1960

me before I went through the trouble of figuring out how I was going to pull this off without a car.

I decided to ask her when we broke for morning break. I cannot tell you how nervous I was. I was nervous about the fact that she might say no, and the feeling of rejection would overwhelm me. Then I was a little nervous about the fact that she might say yes. Then what would I say next? This was a major problem that I would have to work out some way.

When we stopped for our morning break, she started toward the concession stand, and I came up from behind her until I was walking alongside her. My heart was racing and I knew I was going to have a problem saying anything. She glanced at me and made eye contact and that made it worse. I didn't know how to do this, so I just put my arm around her neck and shoulder and said something to this effect: "Hey, do you want to go to a drive-in movie, sometime?"

She looked a little startled because of my approach. She thought just a minute and said, "Can I let you know later?"

I mumbled something like, "Okay." I'm not sure what I said.

Now I was really depressed because I thought I blew it. She told me later that I scared her because I was so forward with her. At afternoon break, she walked up to me and said that she had been talking to her girlfriend Faye and her boyfriend, and that she would be willing to go to the drive-in movie with me if we double-dated and went with them. Hey! That was fine with me. Here I had asked a girl to go to a drive-in movie, and I didn't even have a car. Problem solved!

Our first date turned out great. Edna was a little shy but in a very cute sort of way. She had long, silky brown hair and it was always shiny. She was very pretty and had a fantastic build. Her waist, when I met her, was nineteen inches. I could take my hands, put them around her waist, push a little, and touch my fingers together. She was very curvy, so there was that physical attraction to start with. Even though I was young, I knew that a relationship had to move beyond a physical attraction to be able to flourish.

Edna was living with her sister and brother-in law in Melrose Park, and I was still living with my father and Marie in the Field Avenue house in Broadview. It was great that we worked at the same place because I was able to see her every day at work. We would spend a few minutes together before work, eat lunch together every day, and talk for a few minutes after work. I got almost immediate approval from Ray. He walked past us one day at lunch and gave us a thumbs up. This meant a lot to me at the time.

Chuck would come over several times during the week, and he would take me to pick up Edna and we would go and do fun things together. Sometimes it was going out to eat, sometimes bowling, and sometimes to a movie. I guess most people, when they start having a relationship with someone, really want approval from their friends and their family. I will never forget what Chuck said after the first time we all went out together. We had just dropped Edna off and Chuck turned to me and said, "Wow! You're lucky. She is a living doll." This made me feel good. Chuck was a part of my life for a lot of years, and he and Edna always got along great.

We had a bit of a problem finding some alone time. My father would occasionally let me use his car on week nights, but I had a curfew and knew better than break it or that would be the end of him letting me use it again. On week nights when he let me use the car, I would go over and pick up Edna, and we would mostly ride around or go somewhere and park.

We did a lot of talking as we began to get acquainted. I realized we had a lot in common. Our childhoods had some similarities that helped a lot in the bonding process. Her living conditions were every bit as bad as mine were. Her house was pretty much a shack. They did have some electricity, but, just like us, it was not much. They did not have any running water either. Their well was in the front of the house and fairly close to the house.

They had an outhouse pretty far behind the house. They had a wood-burning cook stove like us, but instead of a potbellied stove, they had an open fireplace for heat. So, you can see, our living conditions were quite similar. Despite these similarities, there were some key factors that made our childhoods completely different. In Mississippi, it rarely snows and rarely gets really cold, so they did not have snow and frigid temperatures to deal with. They did have the heat to contend with, especially cooking on a wood-burning stove when it was a hundred degrees outside.

The major difference in our upbringing was that she had a loving father and mother who stayed together until death. She had two older sisters who were both married at this time — Yvonne, who was married to Billy Wilson, and Betty Sue, who was married to James Gattis. Her only brother, Doyle, was a couple of years older than her and the only one still living at home.

Edna's sister Betty Sue

Her family was very poor, but then again, just about everybody around there was also poor. Her father worked at a sawmill, but I don't think they stayed busy enough for him to work full time. They did have a large garden and also raised hogs and chickens. Edna said they always had food to eat, but not much money.

Edna quit school after her freshman year in high school, mainly to go to work and earn money to buy clothes, etc. She got a job as a waitress in a café in the town of Iuka, Mississippi, and she made enough money to take care of her personal needs and transportation costs, as she had to pay someone to bring her to work and pick her up.

So, here we were, with a lot in common. Both of us were high school dropouts and both of us were raised in poverty. The upside to this is that both of us longed for a better lifestyle, and both of us were willing to work for it.

Somewhere around January 1960, I managed to find a furnished basement efficiency apartment in Bellwood, Illinois, just about one mile from where we worked. I asked Edna to move in with me and that ended the problem of trying to figure out how to make arrangements to see her.

The rent was $17.50 per week. I know that sounds cheap, but Edna was making minimum wage, which was somewhere around $1.00 per hour, and I was making $1.25 per hour. Our take-home pay was somewhere in the $35-40 range per week. It worked out fine. My check would cover the rent and buy a week's groceries.

That left Edna's check for everything else. From that point, until today, I never felt poor again. I was enjoying what I considered a great lifestyle and I was sharing it with someone I loved.

I had what was missing in my life. Edna was a friend, companion, and soon-to-be wife all wrapped into one. I now had more incentive to strive for a better way of life than I ever had before. I had somebody else to work for and we had common goals. The terrible loneliness that had plagued me since my mother passed away was pretty much gone. Yes, a certain sadness continues even to this day, but the horrible loneliness was gone. I felt like I had someone who loved me and cared deeply.

We still had the problem of no car. Let me quote an old Steven Wright joke: *Every place is within walking distance if you have the time.* At least this was a very bearable problem. We could walk to work and back and we were close to shopping, so we could walk to the grocery store, laundromat, and restaurant.

We bought our weekly groceries every Friday night from a Jewel grocery store about two blocks from where we lived. I would come out of the grocery store with my cart full of groceries, walk through the parking lot, and just keep trucking all the way home with the grocery cart. The next time we went, I would get the cart that we had parked alongside the garage, and go back to the grocery store. I used the same cart every week and nobody ever said anything about it.

The laundromat was a different story. We looked long and hard and finally found a nice cart that we could pull behind us to carry our clothes to and from the laundromat. We were able to manage just fine, except we still really wanted a car. We could not go anywhere we wanted, when we wanted, and I guess that is what we missed most.

Life rocked along like this for three or four months. One day, on our way to the laundromat, we decided to look at some cars at a used car lot. I spotted a 1952 Chevy that really looked clean, and they wanted $250 for it. The owner, Tom, who I vividly remember, came out when he noticed us looking at the car. I told him that I did not have the money right now, but I would like to see if I could pay for it with weekly payments. He kind of snapped at me and said, "Do I look like a bank? Go and borrow the money and come back, and I will be happy to sell you the car."

I said something like, "I'll see what I can do." And we walked away. I knew I couldn't borrow $250 from anyone, except maybe Grandma Gallo, but I wasn't ready to throw in the towel just yet. Maybe we could save it up and pay cash for it in time.

We were getting by fine, but starting out, we had to buy a lot of things like dishes, pots and pans, sheets, towels, and all kinds of other things. We had bought most of that, but every time we saved a few dollars, something would come along, like going to the dentist, that would eat up our little savings.

I sure wanted that car. I decided to make one more attempt to buy it. When we got paid on Friday, I felt like I could approach Tom and tell him that I had twenty dollars that I could put down on the car, if he would let me pay fifteen dollars per week until I got it paid off. So here we go back again.

I started looking at the car again and here comes Tom. His first question was, "Were you able to come up with the money?"

I told him that I didn't, but asked him if I could put twenty dollars down and pay fifteen dollars a week until I got it paid off.

He was a little gruff again as he said, "I told you that I was not a bank. I don't sell cars on credit."

I told him I knew that but that I did not know of any other way of doing this, and we really needed a car. I told him where we lived and that we had to walk everywhere we went.

He softened just a little and said. "I understand your situation, but you have to understand mine."

I said I did and we turned and walked away.

We got to the end of the parking lot and he said, "Wait a minute! Come here a second."

I walked back to where he was standing and he said, "How much did you say you could pay a week?"

I told him fifteen dollars.

"Okay, let's go in my office."

He sat me down and told me he would hold the title and expect me to pay fifteen dollars every week, but the first time I missed a payment, he would come and get the car. He explained that he didn't normally do this, but he felt like I would keep my word.

Wow! Wow! And wow! We had a car. After doing some paperwork, he let us drive off with the car. Folks, I cannot tell you how happy we both were. *Imagine that!* We had our very own car. We could go places and do things that we could never do before. This was one of the happier moments in my young life. Even now, I am actually getting excited and happy thinking about it again.

I kept my word and had the car paid off in about four months. There is a little sideline to this story that I would like to interject at this time. One week we had a big expense but I don't remember what it was. Normally every Friday I would go to the lot and hand Tom fifteen dollars. I approached him about seeing if we could skip a week because we were short on money. However, I did have the money in my pocket in case he said no. He first said, "NO! I told you if you missed a payment I would come and get the car."

I said okay and handed him the money.

I turned to leave and just before I walked out the door he said. "Come on back here." When I walked back to his desk, he handed me back the money and said, "Damn you Bill, I don't know why I always give in to you. Just this one time, do you understand?"

I said I did, and thanked him. Below that gruff exterior was a man with a soft heart. When I gave him the last payment, he signed the title over to me and told me that if I ever needed a car again, to come and see him. I kept that in mind and did end up getting another car from him later.

This was in 1960, and from that time until today, I have never been without a car, or two, or three. I am thankful to God for answering my prayers.

When 1959 drew to a close, I think I would have to chalk that up as the most eventful year of my life. I had run away from home. I had gotten my first car (sort of), I had started my first job, I had rented my first apartment for a while, and finally, and most importantly, I went out on my first real date with the girl who would later become my wife. That is a lot of activity for someone who should have been in their senior year in high school. Had I stayed in school I would have graduated from Luther L. Wright High School with the class of 1960.

The small basement apartment that we rented was very nice, except for one major thing. It did not have a bathtub or shower. It had a very large laundry tub in the unfinished part of the basement that we, uncomfortable as it was, were able to get in by sitting on the side of it. What is it about these basements and laundry tubs? It did have a bathroom with a commode and sink. It was basically one large room with a partition between the bedroom area and the kitchen. The kitchen was laid out nicely, with enough cabinet and counter space, a double sink, and a stove and refrigerator. Most ranges in the Chicagoland area are natural gas, as was this one.

We had already committed to each other when Edna moved in. but we both wanted to make it legal by getting married. I found out that in the state of Illinois at that time, you could not get married if you were under the age of twenty-one, unless you had a parent or guardian to sign for you. I don't think it is that way any longer.

We wanted very much to get this done, so I drove over by my-self to approach my father and Marie to see if Father would sign for us to get married. I was surprised by their response and a little hurt, and maybe a little angry.

Marie had always pushed for me to have a relationship with the girl who lived across the street. Her parents were well-respected in the neighborhood and they went to the same church as my father and Marie. The girl also had a beautiful soprano voice and sang at church on numerous occasions. Marie had approached me several times and suggested I ask her out on a date. It was like she thought she was the perfect All-American girl. I did like her, but that was as far as it went.

Marie was visibly angry when I made this request and lashed out at me saying, "You have the perfect girl right across the street and you want to marry some stupid hillbilly! What is wrong with you?"

Father refused to sign and also berated Edna to me by saying, "You are too young to even know what you are doing, or you wouldn't even think about marrying some hillbilly."

That was enough for me. I never said a word, I just walked out. Father followed me out to the car insisting we talk about this. I told him I heard all I wanted to hear and there was nothing else to talk about. When I returned home, I told Edna that my father said he wouldn't sign because he thought I was too young. I did not have the heart to tell her the rest of the story.

After I had a chance to collect my thoughts, I reasoned that this was just a little bump in the road, and that we could work through this situation. It didn't take me long to figure out that I could call my dad in Michigan to see if he would sign for me. After all he was my legal guardian since he was awarded custody of Ray and me in our last custody battle in Bessemer, Michigan. Dad and Johnny had a phone now, and so far, we did not. I went to a pay phone and called him. He seemed happy to hear from me and said that if I was sure that was what I wanted to do, he would gladly sign.

This was great! We would go to Ironwood and get married. That way I could have my friends and relatives present. How cool is that! I qualified for a week's vacation from work and they let me have the second week in July off. Edna had not been there a year, so she did not have a vacation coming. I talked to my supervisor at work and explained what we were doing and asked if they would be able to let Edna off for a week also. I knew it would be with no pay, but I didn't want her to miss work and lose her job. He told me that he would talk to someone in the office and let me know. He came back with the best news. The plant manager agreed and he wanted our supervisor, Harvey, to tell us congratulations. A few days later, he came out and shook my hand and gave Edna a big hug. Some of the people at work took up a collection for us. I can't tell you how grateful we were for that.

We had managed to save a little money and since we were having some mechanical problems with our car, we decided to take the Northwestern train from Chicago to Ironwood. It was really a fun time. We stayed with Uncle Waiko and Aunt Ruth because they had more room.

Times have changed a lot over the years. It was considered very bad if you lived with someone and weren't married, and also it was considered very inappropriate to get intimate with someone until after marriage. Anyway, that was the standard that was set back in those days. So, naturally, I did not tell anyone that we were already living together. Bummer! They made sure we slept in different rooms the whole time we were there.

Edna prior to our marriage, early 1960

I got a pleasant surprise when I applied for our wedding license. I was told that in the state of Michigan, you did not need to have anyone sign if you were eighteen or older. That was great. I was two months past my eighteenth birthday, and Edna was nineteen years old. It also meant that we didn't have to bring Dad down there to sign, since he had a hard time getting around.

All the arrangements had been made and our wedding date was July 9, 1960. My friend Ray Saari, cousins Wesley Ranta and Ruthie Spetz, and my sister Barbara were in the wedding party. The ceremony took place in the living room at Uncle Waiko and Aunt Ruth's house. The Reverend Walter Reini presided. After the wedding was over, we had refreshments and everyone visited for a while. Hand-held cameras were not too good in those days, so our entire wedding party went to Allen's Portrait Studio in Ironwood for our wedding pictures.

I do not remember exactly where we went to celebrate, but it was somewhere in Hurley, and we all had a few drinks. Then it was back to Uncle Waiko and Aunt Ruth's house to pack up. We left that very night heading back to Chicago.

Mr. and Mrs. William Payne
Wedding Day — July 9, 1960

L — R: Cousin Ruthie Spetz, cousin Wesley Ranta, Edna, Bill,
best friend Ray Saari, sister Barbara

Bill and Edna — late 1980s

16 Damn Yankee

THE TRAIN RIDE FROM IRONWOOD back to Chicago was fun. This was the first and only time either one of us ever slept in a Pullman berth. It was really neat — kind of like sleeping on the top bunk of a set of bunk beds. There was a curtain that could be drawn closed for privacy, and it either snapped shut or zipped shut. Anyway, this was our wedding night, and our family had kept us in separate bedrooms since we were there. To say we didn't get much sleep in that Pullman berth would be an understatement.

Chuck was at the Northwestern train station in Chicago to pick us up and take us home. What a friend! We settled back into our routine of working and driving around. We got our car fixed and were on the go visiting my sister Dolly, Ray and Jean, my grandmother, and my cousins. We also met with Chuck to do things. We visited Ray and Jean quite a bit and mostly ate at their house, since we didn't have much room in our small apartment. We also started visiting my father and Marie. Since our wedding was a done deal, they started accepting Edna as my wife, and they were actually quite nice to her. I never did tell her that they were opposed to us getting married. I was willing to put that incident behind me, but I am not so sure Edna would have, if she had known.

To those who were raised in the North as I was, you may not be aware of the prejudice against Southerners that existed back in that day, and probably some exists even now. This prejudice also exists in the South against Northerners. You would be surprised to know that people from the South think that people in the North talk funny. They call it that *Yankee Brogue.*

Edna's father, Buford, had sent a message to Edna through her sister Betty Sue, instructing her to tell Edna that she better not marry one of those damn Yankees. Edna told me about it, and that didn't exactly make me want to go there to meet him, although I knew that was inevitable. We had a car now, and Edna really wanted to go home to see her family and introduce me. She had been corresponding with them through the mail, and they knew that we were married.

We decided to take a quick weekend trip there to see them. We left work on a Friday and drove all night to get there fairly early in the morning.

I was nervous about the whole ordeal. I expressed my concern to Edna about her disobeying her father and marrying a Yankee. Her reply threw me for a loop. She was trying to reassure me about the situation, but her choice of words made it worse as she said, "I don't think he will do anything to you. He might even like you."

I replied, "What do you mean, might? He might kill me."

Her classic answer was, "He has never killed anyone before. The worst thing he ever did was beat a guy with an axe handle, but it didn't kill him. He just had a broken arm and some cracked ribs."

We were already on the road during this conversation and I sure was tempted to turn around, but that really was not an option at this point.

We got there in the wee hours of the morning and decided to go to the café in the town of Iuka, Mississippi, where Edna used to work, and have breakfast. This would give her parents a chance to wake up and get dressed. They knew we were coming. I am going to guess that it was probably ten miles from the restaurant to their house, so we finished eating and headed that way.

Was I nervous? Yes, I was. Here I am eighteen years old, five feet, eleven inches tall, and one hundred forty pounds soaking wet. I felt like I was going into enemy territory. A lot of things were going through my mind like, *I wonder if everybody down here hates Yankees?* If they decided to turn on me, it would be curtains for me. I would be the sole Yankee there, and that was not a very happy thought. I knew the Union had defeated the Confederacy in the Civil War, but it wasn't with one soldier.

When we finally turned into their driveway, the first thing I saw was her mother working in the garden wearing one of those very big sun hats. Their garden was in front of the house. As we pulled in her excited mother, Annie, came running over with a big smile on her face as she grabbed Edna and started hugging her and crying. This went on for a few minutes, and then Edna introduced me as her husband. Her mother, with tears running down her face and trying to force a smile through her tears, said she was happy to meet me. She was a wonderful person. I never heard her ever say anything bad about anybody. She was a very positive and loving mother in law.

Annie grabbed the few tools she was working with as we started walking toward the house. When we got close to the house, I spotted him. There he was sitting in a porch swing slowly rocking back and forth. He had on a cap that looked like a railroad hat and blue jean bib overalls. His hat was pulled down almost to his eyes, and he seemed to just be staring at the floor. Wow! What a menacing looking person he was. My heart was in my throat by this time.

Edna went over to her dad and gave him a hug, and he acknowledged her by just patting her on the back. "Daddy, I want to introduce you to my husband, Bill."

He raised his head a little and looked at me with a very solemn expression, as he said in a very low voice, "What do you say, Boy?"

I wasn't sure what to do next so I said something to the effect of, "Good to meet you," and I stuck out my hand to give him a handshake. He did shake my hand, but it sure didn't seem like it was a very enthusiastic handshake. He never smiled, and he kept looking straight at me with that very solemn look on his face.

That's when Edna announced to me, "Just stay here and talk to Daddy; me and Mother are going into the house."

She didn't understand. I didn't want to stay on the porch and talk to Daddy. I wanted to go in the house, too. There is no telling what Daddy was thinking, but judging by the look on his face, it didn't appear to be anything good. After they went into the house I started to feel kind of awkward because I didn't know what to say.

He finally stood up and said, "Come around back, Boy! I want to show you something."

Now what? He is going to kill me for sure. I was afraid to go with him, but I was more afraid not to. By now I was so weak I could barely walk, but I managed to follow him.

We got around the side of the house and he said, "Look what I got." He reached in his bib overalls, and I was sure he was going to pull out a gun or a knife. But, lo and behold, he pulled out a bottle with a clear liquid in it as he said, "Have you ever had any White Lightnin' before?"

Folks, I was never so happy to see a bottle of liquor in my entire young life. My fear now started turning to excitement as I said, "Oh, sure! I really like it." *Lord, please forgive me for lying!*

Let me put this story on hold for a minute and explain some of the customs in the Deep South, especially in this part of Mississippi. First, when people have company, the women always go into the house and the men always stay outside on the porch. Second, if you were drinking, as the men usually were, you did not do it on the porch in plain view. You always went around to the side of the house, out of sight, to have a drink. Always! The other thing was that if you had company over and you were opening a new bottle, you offered the first drink to your company. These people drank straight out of the bottle with no chaser. Of course, at this juncture, I did not know that.

Okay, I'm back. So, Buford opens the bottle and hands it to me saying, "You are really going to like this. It is the pure stuff. Go ahead and take a big drink."

I was so happy to know that I wasn't going to be beaten or killed that I would have drank the whole bottle if he wanted me to. Wait! On second thought, there is no way I could have drank the whole bottle without passing out. I had already stuck my foot in my mouth by saying I had drank White Lightning and that I liked it. Actually, I had never even seen any of it in my entire lifetime. So, to impress my new father-in-law, I turned the bottle up and took a big drink with a few *glug glugs* in there.

As I was handing him back the bottle, I thought I was going to die. That was the nastiest-tasting stuff I had ever drank, and it burned all the way down my throat and into my stomach. I thought for a minute that it was going to come back up, but luckily it didn't.

"How do you like that stuff, Boy?"

I could barely talk as I said, "That is the best White Lightning I have ever tasted."

On the way home, I asked Edna about the guy that Buford had beaten with an axe handle. Are you ready for this? Her reply was, "I was just kidding about that."

"What?"

"I just thought it was funny to see the expression on your face when I told you that."

Even after I told her that it wasn't funny, she still laughed. Go figure. I informed her that she would never make it as a comedian because her jokes were not funny, especially this one.

My father-in-law, Buford, and I got along great after that. He even took me squirrel hunting one time. That was a cool experience. He had two great squirrel dogs, and all we did was sit on a log smoking a cigarette until the dogs treed a squirrel. The tone of their barking changed when they had one in a tree. Buford would look at me and say, "Let's go, they got one."

He ended up killing six and I killed two. Annie cooked them and we had squirrel and dumplings for supper. I couldn't eat any of them. They looked like rats when I watched Buford cleaning them that afternoon, and that just grossed me out. Fortunately, Annie had cooked a big supper and there was plenty of other food to eat.

When we got back to our little apartment in Bellwood, I began looking for a job that would pay more than we were receiving at J. W. Johnson. We really liked our jobs and had made some good friends there, but the pay wasn't very high and I thought we could do better.

I did find a better job. The name of the company was Mercury Metal Products, and they were willing to hire both Edna and me. It was kind of a boring job, but it paid quite a bit more than we were previously making. We both ran a punch press. When I worked there, I was punching out the wing nuts that secured the spare tire in the trunk of cars. I was ever in search of jobs that paid more.

After working there for several months, my friend Chuck Lawrence told me about a job opening at a plant in Broadview that was called Labeled Metal Products, later to be named Quaker State Metal Products. They paid considerably more than Mercury Metal Products, but they needed only one person. I reasoned that I could take the job and Edna could find another job somewhere else. During those days, manufacturing jobs were easy to find because things were booming in the Chicago area.

Quaker State Metal Products dealt mostly in sheet metal products like gutters and duct work. I went to work in the shearing department. Our department was small, with four of us cutting the sheet metal to size, putting it on skids, and moving it with a forklift truck to the appropriate department. I liked this job better than any of my previous jobs. We were a team, and we would meet and try to figure out how we were going to make deadlines on some of the rush orders that would have to be shipped on certain days. Sometimes the only answer would be to work overtime, which we often did, and I loved it.

It just so happened at about this same time that Ray and Jean moved to a bigger apartment close by. That is when my father and Marie decided to move from the basement of their house to the upstairs apartment that Ray and Jean had vacated, with Al and Coral still on the main floor. They asked us if we wanted to rent the basement. I had lived there before, but it was with them. Now we would have the whole basement. It was not as nice or cute as the apartment we would be giving up, but we did have a little more room, and it was closer to my new job. I could walk to work if need be. Yes, it did not have a bathtub or shower, but then again, neither did the place we were moving from. So back to Broadview we went. Ray and Jean had moved close enough so that I could get to their house by walking from our back yard to theirs. We were surrounded by family and friends — and we were kind of excited about that.

The other nice thing was that Chuck was not far away. His parents had moved to Westchester, a suburb that adjoined Broadview. Chuck's father and mother, Charles and Harriet Lawrence, had kept the house next door, made three apartments out of it, and rented them. Gary Shepherd and his wife Glenda had moved into the middle apartment and were next door to us. We became best friends shortly after that. Gary was a painter and worked for Charles Lawrence along with Chuck and several other guys.

It wasn't long after we moved back to Broadview that I started my new job at Labeled Metal Products. Edna had found a really good job also. Marie had been working at Motorola where they were manufacturing television sets. She helped Edna get a job there and it worked out perfectly. There were two other women from our neighborhood who also worked there, so they were able to carpool. I could use our car to drive to my job, which was maybe six blocks away. Sometimes on nice days I would just walk. Things were going well for us, and we soon started thinking about getting another car.

We were in the later part of 1960, and Edna and I were becoming concerned about the fact that she wasn't pregnant yet. We had only been married about four months, but we had been together for a total of approximately nine months. In those days it was like you were on a mission to get married and have children. That was just what you were supposed to do if you were a normal couple. None of this waiting until you have a house, or finish college, or get a better job. You were just supposed to have a baby and go from there.

I think people in this generation are more practical than we were back then. Edna really wanted to have a baby. Nobody ever explained anything to us about the birds and bees, and we were starting to become concerned. We thought that there must be something wrong with one of us for her not to be pregnant. After all, we were doing everything we knew to make this happen, and it wasn't happening. We finally decided to make a doctor's appointment for Edna to see if she had any kind of problem that would prevent her from becoming pregnant. I decided to go with her.

After they examined her, they consulted with us and assured us that we were still young and that sometimes it just takes time. They wanted us to relax and not stress over it. They really didn't think there was a problem with Edna. I was okay with that but wondered if maybe there was a problem with me. Anyway, we stopped worrying about it or even talking about it for the time being.

Ray had a really good job with the City of Broadview. His main job was trimming trees that would fall on the power lines or that started to grow too close to the power lines. He had a lot of experience working in the woods when he was in Ironwood and was very adept at using a power saw. One day he came over and asked me if I would help him cut down a neighbor's tree. His neighbor had a very large tree in his front yard, and for some reason, wanted it to be removed. Ray, being the nice guy that he was, not only volunteered to do it for nothing, but also volunteered my help. So here we go.

The first thing we did was size up the situation. It was a huge tree and we were going to cut it down, cut it into firewood, and stack it close to the road. Then we were going to cut up the brush and his neighbor was going to take care of any clean up. Simple, but the only way we could drop the tree was toward the road, and there were power lines there.

I expressed concern and said that it looked like it might hit the power lines, but I wasn't sure. Ray's reply was, "Don't you know how to figure that out?"

"No! How?"

"All you have to do is measure the shadow, and once you get that measurement, you measure from the base of the tree toward the power lines and you will know if it will hit the lines or not."

Now I am thinking, *Hmmm!* The shadow is on the back side of the tree toward the house in the opposite direction of where we wanted it to fall. It didn't make much sense because the shadow changes size as the sun moves. But hey! My brother cuts trees for a living, and who am I to question him. I was sure he knew something that I didn't know.

He held one end of the tape against the bottom of the tree, and I measured the shadow. Then we moved to the other side of the tree and used the same measurement toward the power line where we were going to drop it. Lo and behold, according to our measurements the tree was going to fall at least eight feet short of the power lines. How neat is that? I asked Ray how he knew about this method and he told me he had seen them do it at work.

Ray was cutting away and just before the tree fell, he pulled his saw back and hollered, "Timber!"

Damn! I couldn't believe it. It landed right across the power lines and pulled them down.

Ray looked at me and said, "There must have been more to it than this."

The neighbor came out looking pretty bewildered when he saw what had happened. Ray told him to call the city. This was a weekend and they only worked a skeleton crew, but they came in just a short time. They all knew Ray and he knew them as well.

They came over to where we were standing and said, "Ray! What the hell happened?"

He looked at them and said, "We made a little mistake. My brother measured wrong."

164

Not wanting to get my brother into trouble or to maybe lose his job, I just shrugged my shoulders and tried to look stupid. We could have been in serious trouble, but since Ray worked for them, we were forgiven, I guess.

They called the power company and they all worked together, including Ray, to cut up the tree and restore the lines. I had gone home because I was sure they were convinced they didn't need me.

Okay, if you don't remember anything from this story, remember this — if you have a tree to cut down and wonder if it is going to hit anything, *do not measure the shadow. It doesn't work!*

Things were going well for us as we neared the end of 1960. I liked my job at Labeled Metal Products. I was making $2.25 per hour. I know that doesn't sound like much, but the minimum wage was around $1.00 per hour and I was making $1.25 per hour when I quit working at J. W. Johnson Company. I then worked at Mercury Metal Products for a couple of months for $1.50 per hour before moving to Labeled Metal Products for $2.25 per hour. We would usually get four to eight hours of overtime a week, so that added to it. I was feeling pretty good about myself because I had moved up $1.00 per hour in just about one year.

Not long after we turned the corner into 1961, Edna informed me that she thought she was pregnant, so we made an appointment somewhere around the end of January or early February. I will never forget this appointment. After they called her into the examination room, I was trying my best to be patient. I was sitting in the waiting room in anticipation of the outcome.

When she finally emerged, I knew the answer. She was literally beaming. As she approached, I went ahead and asked, "Are you?"

She was smiling when I asked, but that came to an abrupt halt when she answered, "Yes," because at that point she broke down and started crying. They were tears of happiness. Edna had babysat a lot for her sister and other young parents in the countryside when she was living at home. She loved children and

Edna pregnant with Ted, holding brother Ray's daughter Teresa

longed for the day when she would have a baby of her own. I was happy also. Now I knew we were both normal and we would soon be parents. That is part of what I thought marriage was all about.

Let me back up a minute. When my mother passed away giving birth to Ronnie, a lot of people said that she had worked too hard while she was pregnant and some of them, mostly my Italian side of the family, thought that contributed to her death. I am not sure when Dad moved her from the logging camp to the house in Wakefield, but it didn't seem very long. I didn't want that to happen to Edna, so I asked her to go ahead and quit her job.

She really didn't want to and said, "I can work a little longer. I am only about two months pregnant." So, I agreed.

It was not long after that when she started having morning sickness. I didn't know anything about that at the time, but I didn't like it. I put my foot down and had her quit.

She wanted to continue and said something like, "We have a baby coming and we can use the extra money."

I told her not to worry about the money, I could get a second job if need be.

My incentive had shifted into high gear. It was on me to be the breadwinner, and I would be working for three people now. I was determined that we weren't going to be poor like I was when I was growing up. I kicked it up a notch at work and informed my boss, Milton, that if they ever needed anyone to work overtime, I would be willing.

I got along well with Milton and he seemed to like my work ethic. There were only four of us in the shearing department, and it was our job to cut the metal and bring it to different departments for forming and assembly. Milton would get the orders from the office and pass them out to me, Don, and Frank. Don was a few years older than me, and Frank was an older gentleman from Poland who had migrated to this country during World War II. He spoke broken English, but after being around him awhile, I could communicate with him fairly well.

My attendance was perfect for the first full year. They had a meeting and announced the names of the people who had perfect attendance for one year and gave us all a present. I was the only one in my department to be recognized, and, yes, I was feeling good about that.

Milton's health had gone down to the point where he was not able to work full time. The company allowed him to work three days a week and six hours a day. When this happened, I was called into the office and given another twenty-five cent raise. I would be responsible for our department when Milton wasn't there, and now that would be more often. I had to do whatever was necessary for our department to meet all the deadlines.

I relished the added responsibilities. Our plant supervisor called me on the side and asked me not to say anything to anybody about the raise because there were people there who might not like it. I agreed.

This was a happy time in my life. I felt like I was making good money, and I was about to be a father. Things seemed to be changing for the better at a fairly rapid pace. I was just nineteen years old at this point.

Finally! The day came. Charles Theodore Payne was born at Hinsdale Sanitarium and Hospital in Hinsdale, Illinois, on September 16, 1961. The ironic thing was that my mother died on September 16, 1951, and now ten years later to the day, my son Ted was born. I have done a lot of reflecting on that and it makes me think of the saying, *The Lord giveth and the Lord taketh away.* It was almost like God was saying, "Here you go, Bill; I know how sad you were when your mother died, so this is my present to you because I love you."

Baby Ted

Edna's water bag had broken some days before Ted was born, which meant she had a dry birth. Dr. Brayshaw had to use forceps to help pull him out. I was sitting by Edna's bed when they brought the baby to her. She broke down and started crying again, but this time they were not tears of joy. Ted's head looked a little deformed and it scared me also. The nurse immediately informed us that it was no problem. She explained that when a doctor uses forceps it temporarily makes it appear the baby's head is out of shape, and she assured us that this would go away. We breathed a sigh of relief, for sure. He was just fine and weighed in at seven pounds, ten ounces. We had both been up all night, and by now it was mid-morning.

After an hour or so, I decided to go home to get some rest and let Edna rest also. Although I was tired, I was happy. I stopped on my way home and bought a whole box of Cuban cigars that said, *It's a boy*. I ended up passing a few around the neighborhood, Ray included, and the rest at work. What a great day that was.

Here I was a father at nineteen years old. Most kids who went on to college were freshmen at this age. Since I was so young, many years later I would introduce Ted as my son and say, "We grew up together!"

Bill, Ted, and Edna
on Ted's first birthday — 1962

Ted — mid-1990s

17
Movin' On Up

THE YEAR 1961 WAS A good year. Ted was born in September, and a lot of other good things happened as we endeavored to improve our lifestyle for us and our children. It was also the year that we took inventory of our life and agreed that we would like to start attending church and raise our children to be Christians. Edna and I had not been attending church anywhere. Edna's uncle, John Henry Mock, was a Pentecostal preacher in Mississippi, and he pastored a local church called Palestine. That was "The Church" for her entire family and most families who lived in the area.

There was, and still is, a fairly large cemetery across the road from the church. I can't count the number of funerals that I attended at the church. It was customary when someone passed away, that their body would be brought to the church for review the day before the funeral so that appropriate condolences could be offered to the family. People would also visit with others at this time. The body would remain there all night, and the church would be unlocked so that people could come and go as desired. A great deal of care was taken by the family so that a family member would be there at all times. They called it sitting up with the dead.

I know this terminology sounds morbid, but that is the way it was. Almost everyone who came would bring food and leave it in the adjoining kitchen-eating area. The funeral service would take place the next day in the church, and the body would then be brought to the cemetery for the burial service. After that, everyone would return to the church and eat or just hang around and visit. This was Edna's only exposure to Christianity. Her family were not regular church-goers, but this is where they would go when they did attend on special occasions.

Most of my exposure to Christianity was at a very young age. My mother, who was a Seventh Day Adventist, took us to church every Saturday without fail. When she passed away, we stopped attending. Later, when we moved to Ironwood Township, I went with cousins and friends to people's houses for catechism classes. Sometimes we would attend St. John's Lutheran Church located at Hautala's Corner in Ironwood Township. This was the extent of my exposure to church and Christianity.

Edna and I had long talks about Christianity and the fact that we both believed in God, and in the Christian faith in particular. We jointly made a decision that especially now that we had a child, we should join a church and start attending regularly as a family.

Good friend Gary Shepherd with daughter Sandy — 1968

There was a Christian church a block away that most of our neighbors attended, so we decided to go there and see how we liked it. Our neighbors, Gary and Glenda Shepherd, belonged to the church along with my friend Chuck Lawrence, his mother and father, and his entire family. A new pastor had just taken over and had purchased a house on the same block as ours. His name was Joseph Dobias. He was from Czechoslovakia, but spoke fluent English. His wife, Libby, was American. Their son David was away at college. They also had a son Freddy, who had died at a young age. In addition, they had an adopted daughter named Doris, who was about ten years old at this time.

We really liked the church, the people, and especially the pastor and his wife. When I first met Pastor Dobias in the lobby of the church, he looked at me and said, "I can't believe it."

He then turned to Libby, who was standing a few feet away talking to some ladies, and said, "Come here, Libby, and meet Bill!"

When she approached, he said, "Who does Bill look like?"

She looked a little startled as she exclaimed, "Oh my! He looks almost exactly like Freddy!"

The pastor replied, "That is what I was thinking. I can't believe how much he looks like Freddy before he died." I never did ask them how he died, but I knew he was about my age when he passed away.

This little incident led to a very strong bond that Edna and I had with them for approximately the next five years. He immediately wanted to get me involved in the church, and after attending there for several months, he asked me to be the Young People's Leader. I told him that I didn't think I was ready for that. He encouraged me by saying that he would be there to help out wherever and whenever I needed him. My job consisted of planning clean, fun entertainment for the youth in the church and trying to get other young people involved in church activities. I would often have to get up in front during the service to make announcements. At first, I was a little apprehensive, but after several times, I was okay with it.

During the next five years, we became close friends with Gary and Glenda. I mean, really close! One week after church they would eat at our house, and the next week we would eat at their house. We went everywhere together, even vacations. What a great couple they were. They lived next door, and we would walk back and forth whenever we felt like we wanted to talk to one of them, and they would do the same. Gary was a painter who worked for Charles Lawrence, Chuck's dad. He was very instrumental in getting me into the painting business later on.

Sometime during 1961, I decided I wanted to buy another car — and not just any car! I wanted a Cadillac. We had started buying some things on credit, like a TV and stereo. I figured that since I had been steadily employed and had a bit of credit history, I should be able to buy a car on credit. I was right.

Edna and Ted
1962

For those of you too young to remember, Cadillac set the standard in luxury cars

171

back in the day. There were no cars like Lexus, Infinity, Acura, or any other car that could be considered its equal. In my young mind, I considered it a status symbol. If you drove a Cadillac, you had arrived, or at least I thought so at the time

When I was growing up, I used to hate helping Dad work on his old cars in below freezing weather. Just trying to get them to start was such a hassle when I was so cold that I felt numb. Dad didn't have much patience with me and would scream at me if he asked for a certain wrench out of the toolbox and I brought him the wrong one. On a few occasions he would throw it at me, but fortunately he never hit me. I had vowed to myself that if I was able to afford a car, it would be a fairly decent one that didn't need to be repaired all the time. I associated working on cars with unhappy moments in my life, and I never was interested in doing any mechanic work.

Of course, I was not contemplating buying a new Cadillac. I couldn't afford that. I had my eyes set on a 1955 Coupe de Ville that was on Tom's used car lot. Yes, this was the same Tom who helped me purchase my first car, even though I didn't have any credit. Tom was happy to see me, especially when I told him I thought my credit would be sufficient to be able to buy this car. He told me that I had come a long way since he first met me and that he was proud of me. He helped me fill out a credit report and took our '52 Chevy in trade. This would be the third time he would be selling this same car. Even though the Caddy was six years old, it was clean as a pin and appeared to have been well taken care of. When Edna and I drove it, we were blown away that it was so big, comfortable, and easy to handle.

Bill proud as a peacock
Broadview — 1963

Okay, let me portray my immaturity at the time. Folks, when I drove off that lot in that Cadillac, I had this exhilarating feeling that I had arrived. Here was this poor kid from Ironwood Township who was nineteen years old, with a wife and baby, an assistant foreman at work, Young People's Leader at church, and driving my own Cadillac. Life just couldn't possibly be any better than this. I stopped and bought a cigar, and I didn't even smoke at this time. I felt that in order to play the role, I needed a cigar. I never lit it. I just put it in my mouth and pretended that I was a man of means. The low esteem I had while growing up because of the loss of my mother and the severe poverty that I had been subjected to, had started to vanish, and I had begun gaining some confidence that maybe I might turn out to be somebody after all.

The first thing we did was head up to Ironwood on the weekend to see Dad, Barbara, and Johnny. I drove in the yard with my head high, realizing I wasn't the poorest kid in the neighborhood any longer.

Dad and Bill checking out the Caddy
Ironwood Township — 1962

Then it was time to go to Mississippi in our new Caddy. When we arrived in Mississippi, we stayed with Edna's sister Betty Sue and her husband, James.

So, on this particular Saturday night in December 1961, James and Betty Sue, two of their friends, Phillip and Mildred, and Edna and I, decided to go to the next county where an American Legion center was located and we could drink and dance. Tishomingo County, where they lived, was a "dry county." We were going to celebrate Betty Sue's birthday which fell on December 14th. She would be turning twenty-five. I was nineteen at the time and Edna was twenty. We had no problem getting in or being served. I remember it being a fun night and everyone was dancing, drinking, and having a good time, or at least we thought we were.

When the Legion center closed, we got in our car and headed home. After we left the neighboring county and drove back into Tishomingo County, we decided to stop in Boonville, Mississippi, and get a bite to eat and coffee before heading home. We were now back in a dry county, and I suppose we were a little loud, as most people are when they have been drinking. We were not in the restaurant long before something happened that would lead to unfortunate circumstances for all of us.

I am not sure exactly why, but it seems like when most women use the rest room they want to be accompanied by another woman. In any event, James and I were sitting on one side of a booth and

Edna and Bet were on the other side. Phillip and Mildred were sitting at a small table next to us. So Edna and Bet decided to go to the bathroom together. At this time, James tapped me on the shoulder and pointed behind us. I turned and there were two young ladies who we recognized as being at the American Legion drinking and dancing while we were there. So, both of us turned around and started talking to them. I was glad I was on the inside of the booth. James made the mistake of putting his hand on the girl's shoulder when he was talking to her.

Edna's sister Betty Sue and husband James Gattis

Then out of nowhere Bet and Edna appeared. Betty Sue, who was a very strong lady at five feet, ten inches and about one hundred fifty pounds, hauled off and slapped poor James right across the face. She also had a few choice words for him. That was it! Some guy came over and told us to leave. I believe they also called the police.

I will never forget when we got outside, Bet and Edna were doing double-time heading for the car, and James and I were casually walking with Phillip and Mildred behind us.

James turned to me and said, "Hey Bill! Why did she hit me?"

I told him that I thought she was jealous of him and that girl he was talking with. I still remember the look of shock on his face as he countered, "But, why? I was just trying to make a new friend."

I answered, "Maybe it was because you had your hand on her shoulder?"

"I don't remember having my hand on her shoulder."

"Well, you did."

"Why didn't you tell me not to do that?"

Oh, the mentality of people when they are drinking!

I was driving, and as soon as we pulled out on the road, blue lights started flashing behind us. Looking back now, it was almost comical, but certainly not at the time. We pulled over and two Boonville policemen walked up to the car and asked us to get out.

Now, if anyone has seen *Smokey and the Bandit*, you will understand this part. Another police car pulled up facing us, and two other police officers got out. One of them was the Chief of Police. He was fat and had a cigar and wore glasses. Sound familiar?

The first thing they did was give us a sobriety test. Betty Sue, who was still blazing mad at James, proceeded to cuss the officer who was trying to administer the test. They immediately placed her under arrest and handcuffed her. They gave James the test and he passed, as did Edna, Mildred, and I. Not so with Phillip. He was staggering around and was arrested for public drunkenness.

Now they turned their attention to searching our car. They would be looking for any alcoholic beverages because it was a dry county and carried stiff penalties for possession.

Let me stop here a moment and explain something. James Meredith had enrolled at the University of Mississippi and became the first black person ever admitted to that university. His struggle with enrollment had been going on for almost a year at this time. He had applied at the very start of 1961 when President Kennedy had taken office. So far he had not been accepted. It wasn't until 1962 that, because of federal intervention, he was finally accepted. Most residents in Mississippi did not like the fact that the government was getting involved in a problem that they perceived was a state problem. They blamed all of this on Northern agitation, in particular the NAACP, which was located in Chicago.

So now you have yours truly driving a car with Illinois tags and from Chicago, no less. There was no way any of this was going through my mind at the time. It is only in hindsight that I am offering this information.

The first thing they asked me to do was open the trunk of my car. Then they proceeded to search our suitcases. I was getting irritated because I thought they were supposed to ask if they could search my car. I did manage to keep my mouth shut to this point. I got a little nervous when they started searching inside the car, because I knew we had bought a six-pack to take home when we left. James must have seen my concern because he looked at me and winked. I eased over closer to him, and he informed me that he had thrown it in the ditch when we started to pull over. I felt like giving him a hug! Now, I was about to learn a very valuable lesson.

They proceeded to snatch Edna's purse that she had on her shoulder and started looking through it, hoping she might have a pint of liquor in it. That is when I opened my big mouth. "Hey, what gives you the right to snatch my wife's purse and strew our luggage all over the place?"

One of them replied, "Buddy, we can do whatever we want when you are under arrest."

Here comes one of the most stupid statements I had ever made in my young life. I said, "Nobody told me I was under arrest."

They smiled and said, "Buddy, you are under arrest." Two of the officers slammed me across the hood of the car while another one cuffed me so tight, I later felt like my hands were going to fall off. They threw me in back of the patrol car with Betty Sue and Phillip. James, Edna, and Mildred followed us to the jail in my car.

While we were on the way, I asked, "What am I being charged with?"

They answered, "Don't worry, we will think of something."

A wave of depression came over me as I realized I was handcuffed in the back of a police car and headed for jail. I had never been arrested or put in jail before, and I sure did not like the thought of it.

When we got to the jail, they informed us that we would have to stay four hours, and that Edna, James, and Mildred could then come back and pick us up. I asked again what I was being charged with, and they again told me that they would think of something because they were not sure at this point.

Four hours later the Chief comes with his cigar to let us out. He told me at that time that I was charged with interfering with an officer. He said that if I could come up with fifty dollars, they would forget the whole thing. I had given my billfold to Edna and she was there. Fortunately, I did have enough money, so she got it out of my billfold and handed it to them. I am not sure what Betty Sue and Phillip had to do or pay. They were charged with public drunkenness, and I don't think it was as much.

What a humbling experience this was for me and what a lesson I learned. Sometimes it doesn't matter what is right or wrong. It just matters how you handle the situation. I probably wouldn't have been arrested if I had just kept quiet.

Oh, by the way! Edna, James, and Mildred had gone back to pick up the beer that was thrown in the ditch, and James had it iced down in the cooler when they picked us up. How brave or how stupid was that?! Here we were in front of the police station with an illegal substance in my car. He asked me as we were driving off, "Hey Bill, do you want a cold beer?"

"No thanks, James."

Edna had two sisters, Yvonne and Betty Sue, and one brother, Doyle. Yvonne and Betty Sue, who were both older than Edna, were already married when we got married. Yvonne had married Billy Wilson and they had four children: Sharon, Karen, Tammy, and Mark. Betty Sue had married James Gattis and they had three children: Michael, Teresa, and Debbie. Doyle married Barbara Gann several years after we got married. They had two children: Nita and Randy.

There you have it — my new Mississippi family. What a great family they were. I loved all of them very much and consider myself so blessed to have married into this family. We were very close. They were people who did not have much, but they were a happy, loving, kind, and loyal family. They lived by an unwritten rule that you did not speak badly or gossip about anyone in the family.

Edna and her siblings were all married just one time — there was no divorce ever in the family. Not one time do I ever recall any of us saying an unkind word to another. Over the years we spent a lot of time together. We traveled there many times, especially after we moved to Chattanooga in 1967. It was just a four-hour drive at that time. We would visit them, and they would come to visit us. Our children would spend several weeks there in the summer, and their children would come to our house. We also spent a lot of holidays and vacations together.

At first, I hesitated to tell the following story because it involved my brother-in-law, Doyle. I want to be sure that everyone understands that education and intelligence are two separate factors. Doyle had very little education. I think he quit school in the fourth grade, but he was a very intelligent man, despite his lack of knowledge on certain subjects. He was a good mechanic and a steady worker, and provided for his family. I have been challenged, when I told this story before, as to the truthfulness of it. Trust me, it is a true story.

We were in Mississippi for the Christmas holidays one year and were staying with Edna's sister, Yvonne. Their mother, Annie, was living with Yvonne after Buford passed away. I did not know it at the time, but when they announced the weather on the radio and gave the wind chill factor, Doyle thought they were saying "Windshield Factory." So here we are sitting around one December morning and in walks Doyle. He was on his way to work and stopped in to say hi. It was a chilly morning, so I made the statement to Doyle, "It's cold out there, isn't it, Doyle?"

His reply was, "Yeah, but not as cold as it is at the Windshield Factory. I don't know exactly where that place is, but it is always colder there than it is here. Looks like whoever owns that place would get them ole boys some heat. Shoot! I wouldn't work there. A feller could freeze to death in no time."

That struck me as very funny, but the concern on his face kept me from laughing out loud. I didn't want to say anything to embarrass him, so I just nodded in agreement.

That got me to thinking. I wonder how long the term wind chill factor has been around. I don't remember it as a kid growing up in Ironwood Township. However, I could stand corrected.

Doyle and I became very close over the years and later he and Barbara managed to purchase some acreage and a house. Doyle had a steady job working on the roads for Tishomingo County. He always seemed to have a few animals. At times he would raise hogs and chickens, and one time he even had a mule. His garden was huge. I would guess it was around an acre. He raised everything, including watermelons and cantaloupes. Whenever we visited in the summer, he would load us up with fresh fruits and vegetables from his garden.

Doyle is the one who introduced me to polk salad. Edna already knew about it and liked it. He gave us a big mess of it, and we took it home for Edna to cook. It was great, and I have loved it ever since. First you boil it. Then you fry it with eggs and onions and add a little garlic salt. Yum! Yum!

I learned how to recognize it, and just about every spring I would find enough to pick a mess. So, we would end up having it once or twice a year. It grows wild and is usually found in dirt that has been turned over, like in a subdivision where roads have recently been put in, especially at the end of a cul-de-sac.

Doyle had some funny expressions, and I loved to hear him talk. One day as we were sitting around, he said, "Bill, do you know anyone who might have an old pick-up for sale? Mine is on its last leg. It doesn't need to be all that great. I just need something to get me backwards and forwards to work."

Did I correct him? Not a chance! He was like a brother to me, for sure. Now, as I am getting older and thinking about writing a book, I think about Doyle and the many memories we shared, and also how I could never write a book about my life without including him in it. Thanks for the memories, Doyle. I believe we will meet again someday.

Bill, Ted and Edna at a ball game
Milwaukee County Stadium — 1964

There was still one problem that I wanted to correct, and that would involve moving again. We were still in the basement apartment at the Field Avenue house in Broadview, Illinois, and we still did not have a bathtub or shower. I started watching the shopper paper in our area and finally found an apartment that we really liked. It was in a new complex and very nice, and was located in a neighboring suburb called North Riverside. We had our eyes on a two-bedroom, one-bathroom apartment on the second floor.

However, there was a small problem. It was unfurnished, and we did not own furniture. I was making fairly good money for a factory worker, and we owned some small items, but not furniture. Edna was not working now, and I did not want her to work. I was old school and thought the mother needed to stay home with the children. We had recently purchased the Cadillac, and I had put a substantial down payment on it. We would also have to come up with two months' rent (the first and last). I knew there was no way that we could afford to buy the furniture it would take to furnish this apartment, but I thought this was something we needed to do.

After giving it some thought, I decided that we needed to go shopping to determine how much money we would need to pull this off. There was a fairly large furniture store in Chicago called Polk Brothers, and we decided to go there. We already had a nice crib for Ted and that would be all we needed for his bedroom.

Here was the list that we made up and decided to price out: double bed with mattress and box spring, dresser and chest of drawers, kitchen table and chairs, couch and chair, coffee table, two end tables, and two lamps. One of the salesmen ran us up the total and it was right at eight hundred dollars.

That was a lot of money and there was no way we had that much. At $2.75 an hour, I was netting one hundred dollars a week. I did feel it was important to somehow bite the bullet and do this. If we didn't buy our own furniture, we would be doomed to continue to rent only furnished apartments, and they were much higher in price than unfurnished ones.

I decided to call my grandmother Gallo and see if I could come over and talk to her about this problem. She consented and was very nice over the phone. I determined that I would ask her if she could loan us the money. I already had a plan to present to her about the terms of paying her back, if she consented to the loan.

Okay, so here I go to see my grandmother. I was very anxious about this because I knew it was a lot of money and my ego was getting in the way. I just felt like I wasn't doing enough, or I wouldn't have to borrow money from my own grandmother. I also wondered how depressed I would be if she said no.

Bill and Grandma Gallo
early 1990s

Grandma Gallo was a very direct person, and although I wasn't sure how she was going to react to my request, I was very sure that she wouldn't beat around the bush. When I got there, she gave me a big hug and told me that she was glad to see me. We both sat down and made a little small talk before I got around to asking her for the money. I told her that I needed eight hundred dollars. But when I attempted to tell her why, she got up and walked over to me, put her hand over my mouth, and said in her broken English: "Itsa no matter why you needa money. You say you needa, I believe you needa."

She got up and said that she would be right back. She went into her bedroom, and in a few minutes came back with eight $100 bills and handed them to me. I hugged her and thanked her for her kindness. I was going to explain that I would pay her eighty dollars per month until I paid her back. She told me I could pay her back any way I wanted and that she was not worried about it. I couldn't wait to get home to tell Edna that the dream we had of moving into a new apartment with all of our own furniture would become a reality, thanks to Grandma Gallo.

The first month I came up with a hundred dollars instead of eighty dollars. I thought I would surprise her by going to her church, sit with her, and then hand her the money after the service. I was feeling pretty good about the fact that I was able to come up with a hundred dollars. After church, I asked her to step to the side, and I attempted to hand her the hundred-dollar bill. She wouldn't take it. She told me that she loved all her grandchildren, and that I could keep the money as a gift. I was stunned and had a bit of a time trying to maintain my composure. We had already bought the furniture and moved into our new apartment. I will never forget this act of kindness by Grandma Gallo.

Years later, my Uncle Joe had a big birthday party for Grandma Gallo in West Palm Beach, Florida. She had turned one hundred years old, and Uncle Joe had rented a big ballroom, hired a band, furnished a meal, and had an open bar for everyone. He loved his mother and wanted everything to be first class. Although she was a hundred years old, she could still get around pretty well.

After the meal was over and the band started playing, I went over to where Grandma Gallo and Uncle Joe were sitting and asked her to dance. She smiled and got up, and we danced a really pretty waltz. When I escorted her back to her chair, she smiled and thanked me, and said that I really made her feel good.

She was now living in Lake Worth and had her own house, but Uncle Joe kept a very close watch over her. I did get to see her often over the years before finally attending her funeral in March of 1995. She lived to be one hundred three years and six months old. I loved my Grandma Gallo.

Back: Cousin Jimmy, Bill, cousins Joey and Bobby, brother Johnny
Front: Sisters Dolly and Barbara, cousins Kathleen and Charmaine
at Grandma Gallo's funeral — 1995

Bill — early 1980s

Sister Dolly, Bill and Edna
in the North Carolina
Mountains — 1980s

Edna and Bill — 1987

182

18 Field Avenue

ONE DAY EARLY IN 1963, Pastor Dobias approached me after the church service and informed me that the people who lived upstairs of their home had moved out. He wanted to know if Edna and I would like to rent it. The pastor and his wife, Libby, had bought the house at the end of Field Avenue when he took over the Broadview Seventh Day Adventist Church. They lived on the main floor, and the upstairs apartment was already rented when they bought the house. I was happy where we were living in North Riverside, but I did miss the old neighborhood. In addition, Pastor Dobias offered us a deal that we couldn't turn down. He offered to rent it to us for half the rent we were paying in North Riverside.

Field Avenue was kind of a unique dead-end street. It was less than a city block long with only four houses on each side of the street. The end of the street bordered the Forest Preserve, and it was always shady there. The house that my father and Marie owned, where we had lived, was the second house on the left. The Dobias' house was the fourth (last) house on the right. Everyone on that street knew one another. We were all friends, like one big family. I told the pastor that we would talk it over, and I would let him know the following day.

Our house on
Field Avenue

Edna wavered a little about the situation, but she liked the idea of moving close to Gary and Glenda, who lived in the third house on the left. We would lose one month's rent if we moved before our lease was up, but we would have that back in two months because of the cheaper rent.

It was an older home, but very nice. Our upstairs apartment had a very large living room with a bay window overlooking the end of the street and the Forest Preserve. There were two bedrooms and a fairly large bathroom with a bathtub. The kitchen was average sized. It also had a really nice back deck, something we didn't have at the apartment we were living in. It really wasn't a step down in quality from where we were staying, and at one-half the rent, we just couldn't turn it down. Another thing we liked was that we were at the end of a dead-end street, which would be a much safer place for Ted to play. The lot was fairly big and had a nice

Edna at home in our
Field Avenue house

front and back yard that was more conducive to raising a child. It sure was nice to have our own furniture since this apartment was unfurnished. I know we were moved in by my twenty-first birthday, which was May 9, 1963, because we have a picture of me holding my birthday cake while sitting on the railing of our back deck. This would be our home for the next four and a half years, and many positive things happened during that time span.

At work, Milton was having health problems and had lost quite a bit of weight. He was unable to work full time, but the company let him work six hours a day, three days a week. This put more responsibility on me, since I would be in charge about half the time. They called me into the office and gave me another twenty-five cent hourly pay raise because of my added responsibility. I was now making $3.00 an hour.

I immediately started thinking of a new car. Edna and I had talked it over and decided we wanted a new Chevy Corvair. We both thought they were cute, and reasoned that it would be the right size for our small family. This would be our first new car, and we were excited. I liked my Cadillac, but it was eight years old and had close to 100,000 miles on it. Cars back in the day did not last as long as they do now. You were lucky if you got 100,000 miles on a car. I reasoned that it was time to lay the old Cadillac to rest.

One thing that bothered me was that the Caddy was paid for, and buying a new car meant going into debt. I say it bothered me, but not for long. I wanted a new Corvair. We did have excellent credit at this point, and I knew that we would have no problem obtaining a loan. When we got to the Chevy dealer, the salesman talked me into buying a 1963 Corvair Monza that was slightly used. It only had 4,000 miles on it, and it was such a huge savings over buying a brand new model that we took it. This turned out to be a big mistake — I mean a really big mistake.

At first, I liked the car. It was like a little hot rod and we could just zip around town. We immediately took a trip to Ironwood in it and then later to Mississippi. Soon after that the troubles started. One day we drove through a slightly flooded street, and water came through the floor board. I was also having trouble keeping the front end aligned. I had it aligned at least three times in the one year we owned it. I took it to a mechanic to see if he could figure out why the water came in and why I couldn't keep it aligned. That was when he laid this bombshell on me. He said the car had been wrecked badly, and the frame had been welded in the front.

The feelings of anger I felt at that time were directed more toward myself than anybody else. I wanted to kick myself for not buying a brand new car like I had set out to do in the first place. The other thing was that the spark plugs had to be changed every 6,000 miles. Yes, I am serious. After about 6,000 miles, the car would start missing and chugging along like a man out of breath. I didn't attribute this problem to the fact that the car had been wrecked, I just concluded that this car was a piece of junk.

About this time, my friend Gary Shepherd asked me to help him with painting on some side jobs he had picked up. He worked full time for Charles Lawrence, along with Chuck and two or three other painters. I jumped at the chance. He seemed to pick up a side job about once a month, and I enjoyed working with him. He taught me a lot about the painting trade. Since we both belonged to the Seventh Day Adventist Church, we would work Sundays whenever possible, along with some evenings through the week.

There were a few weeks I made as much helping Gary as I did at my regular job. He always encouraged me by saying that I had good eye/hand coordination and I was a fast learner. This really kicked my incentive up another notch as I began to realize that learning a trade, given that I was a high school dropout, was a good thing. I liked going from job to job. Some were interior jobs and some were exterior. I enjoyed working outside on nice days. It was a refreshing change from working in the factory on a concrete floor all day.

This rocked along for about a year. I continued working my regular job, but I really enjoyed working side jobs with Gary. The year 1963 was a good year financially, except for buying the Corvair. I had turned twenty-one and was making $3.00 an hour on my regular job and doing well working with Gary part time.

We really liked our apartment on Field Avenue. We were within walking distance of my brother Ray and his wife Jean, Gary and Glenda, my father and Marie, and Coral and Al. We were becoming friends with Jim Mott and his wife Bobbie. I knew Jim when we were kids and he lived with his parents. He was now the owner of the house. They lived in the last house on Field Avenue, straight across the street from us. Gary's wife, Glenda, was Jim's sister so we were a close-knit group.

Dr. Collins, who became our primary care doctor, lived in the second house on the right with his wife and three lovely daughters. Dr. Collins and his wife, Lina, had come to America from Chile.

John and Mary Penn lived in the third house on the right and next door to us. They had two daughters, Elaine and Karen. They went to the same church as we did. This is where Ray and I cut down the tree and crashed it on the power lines.

I loved the time we lived in that neighborhood. Every time I get to Chicago to visit family, I always go to Field Avenue and slowly drive up and down the street a few times. So many good memories come rushing through my mind that I have to pull over and bow my head in gratitude to God for seeing me through the hard times and rewarding me with the good times. The year 1963 had ended, and it was a wonderful year. But 1964 had more surprises in store for us, surprises that would make it even better.

The year 1964 was a monster year for us. It was a life-changing year in many ways. It was the year that saw me turning twenty-two years old. I had a relentless drive and determination to succeed in life, and I was willing to work hard to get there. It came from being raised poor, living in poverty, being raised without a mother, and being totally unhappy for a number of years.

I would like to take a moment and examine some of the old adages that we all like to quote at times. How about this one: *Money can't buy happiness!* There is truth in that, but it is a little misleading. First, happiness is not for sale, but the flip side is that *Poverty sure can't buy happiness either.*

How about this one: *There is nothing wrong with being poor, as long as you are happy.* I never thought this made any sense at all. There is everything wrong with being poor, especially if you don't have much food to eat, clothes to wear, and you are totally confined to home because you have no money or transportation to go any where. In my case, after losing my mother, there was no formula that would have caused me to be happy other than lifestyle changes that came from getting married, having my own family, and adopting a completely different set of priorities.

I think, in my particular case, it was the total frustration that came from being in a very bad situation and not being able to do anything about it. No amount of effort that I could put forth as a child or young teenager could have possibly changed anything. I reasoned that the only way out of my unhappy life would be to go to work. I know people like to say: "Money isn't everything." That may be, but it takes money to buy food, clothes, and shelter. Let's not underestimate the importance of money.

I did feel pretty good about the strides I had made to this point in my life. One of the first things I did in 1964 was to trade in my previously-severely-wrecked 1963 Corvair for a brand new 1964 Buick Special. It was a nice car, a six-cylinder with an aluminum block engine and a stick shift on the column. The first thing they asked me after inspecting my Corvair was, "Has this car been wrecked?" When I replied yes, that gave them the leverage they needed to offer me as little as possible on a trade-in. Yes! I lost my shirt on that deal, but I just wanted to get rid of that cute car which had become ugly really fast.

Here again, I felt good driving off the lot in a new Buick — our very first really new car! Yeah team! It was a silver-bluish color, and we both really liked it. This car never did disappoint me. I liked it until the day I traded it in a few years later.

Okay, now it was time for one really tough decision. I was rolling along at my job with Quaker State Metal Products. I was making $3.00 an hour and doing side jobs with Gary, with no intention of changing anything as far as my employment was concerned. However, circumstances changed that caused me to have to make a decision.

My friend Chuck Lawrence stopped by and said that one of the guys on their painting crew had quit and he had put in a good word for me. He thought his father, Charles Lawrence, would hire me if I went and talked to him. I knew Charles fairly well because we went to the same church where he was one of the elders. I told Chuck that I would give it some serious thought, talk to Edna about it, and let him know.

Just a short time later, here comes Gary Shepherd. He did not know that Chuck had talked to me, and he told me basically the same thing, except he added that he had informed Charles that I had been working with him on side jobs and did have some valuable experience. I asked Gary what kind of pay I could expect if I went to work for Charles Lawrence full time. He told me that Charles usually started paying an apprentice $2.00 an hour, but since I had experience and he needed someone desperately, he would start me off at $2.50.

Wow! This was a really tough decision. I talked to Edna about it, and she did not like the idea at all. She could not understand why I would want to quit my job making $3.00 an hour and take one making $2.50 an hour. She also reasoned that Milton was sick and that it probably wouldn't be long before I would be heading up the shearing department, making even better money than I was now. I told her that I needed some time to think and decided to get in my new Buick and drive to the Forest Preserve Park, a few miles away, and just think on this for a while.

There was no one there when I arrived, so I bowed my head and talked audibly to God. I told Him that He had led me this far, and I really needed Him to help me with this decision. All of a sudden, it was like a light bulb went off in my head and everything seemed really clear as to what I should do. It was like my reasoning power was intensified. It came to me that I had two choices right now, and only two. I could stay working in a factory and spend the rest of my life working in a factory, or I could quit my job and learn a trade. I felt like learning a trade was just as valuable as a college degree. Now, suddenly, it seemed like a no-brainer.

When I got home, I informed Edna that I was going to take the painting job working for Charles Lawrence and that I would be working with Gary and Chuck. Now that I had made up my mind, I started getting excited about working with my two best friends. I started thinking about the potential where I could perhaps go on my own some day after learning the trade.

Edna did not share in my enthusiasm. She let me know that she thought I was making a big mistake. I tried to console her by talking positively about my prospects and potential as a painter. She wasn't buying it and started crying. Now my enthusiasm started to diminish. I was feeling badly because I wanted her to be happy, and I needed her support in this decision.

She noticed the change in my countenance because she stopped crying and looked at me and said, "You really want to do this, don't you?"

I told her, "Yes."

Then she replied, "I think you are making a mistake, but I am going to stand with you anyway because I may be wrong. Go for it." Yes! This was music to my ears for sure. It took her probably six months or so after Quaker State Metals had shut down their Broadview plant, to finally say that she was wrong and that I had done the right thing.

And now for the biggest highlight of the year. I am going to guess it was probably in March that Edna had returned from a doctor's visit with our neighbor, Dr. Collins. He had confirmed the fact that she was pregnant again. What a year this was and it wasn't over yet. My second son, William Timothy (Tim) Payne, was born on November 15, 1964, at the same place that Ted was born — Hinsdale Sanitarium and Hospital.

Tim and Ted on the front steps of our Field Avenue house

Dr. Collins took care of the delivery. It was a perfect delivery with no complications, and he was born a healthy and normal child.

189

These were monumental and life-changing events in 1964. I quit my factory job, took a job as a painter, we bought a new 1964 Buick Special, and our second son, Tim, was born.

One more monumental event happened during this same year. We were living in the upstairs apartment of Pastor Dobias and his wife, and we really enjoyed it. One morning I came bounding down the steps and noticed Pastor Dobias with a small sledge hammer, pounding a stake in the yard that had a *For Sale by Owner* sign on it. I will never forget this scene. Pastor Dobias was struggling a bit because the ground was hard. I offered to help him, but he replied that he could manage it. He did manage to penetrate the ground and it was finally taking hold.

I was surprised so I asked him, "Are you going to sell your house and move?"

He told me he was and that he was planning on telling me when I got off work that day. I was saddened a bit because I thought they were wonderful people. He also told me that he was going to put a clause in the contract that the new owner would have to honor the lease that he had with us.

I was very open with him as I said, "Pastor Dobias, we are going to miss you and Libby and Doris. We love this old house, and if I had the money, I would buy it myself."

"Would you really like to buy this house, Bill?"

"Well, yes, but I do not have the money for a down payment."

He stopped pounding, pulled out the stake, and laid it on the ground, as he said, "If you want this house, it is yours. You don't need a down payment. I own the house and I will sell it to you without a down payment and hold the first mortgage. I will talk to Libby, and if you and Edna can stop over after work today, we will work out the details."

I couldn't believe my ears. Could it be possible that we would soon have our own house? It sure seemed that way.

Needless to say, it was really hard for me to concentrate on work that day as it kept running through my mind about what we would do if we became owners of the house. I did know for sure that we would want to move down to the main floor and rent out the upstairs.

Pastor Dobias was one of the nicest, kindest, and most humble men I have ever met in my life. He had a tremendous influence on me. When he came to Broadview, the members of the church were meeting in the auditorium of their church school, just a block away from where we lived. Pastor Dobias almost immediately initiated a building fund to build a church. He was a great promoter and managed to raise the funds needed, and the small congregation was able to build a new church next to the school.

We loved our pastor and our church family, many of whom were our neighbors. Pastor Dobias had accepted a call in some other state and told me later that he thought his job here at Broadview was complete. He had accepted new challenges somewhere else. We had a farewell dinner for him, and the site was completely packed with people.

Ted in front of *our* house

I came home from work that day and told Edna all about it, and she agreed to go with me to talk to Pastor Dobias and Libby about buying the house. What a nice meeting we had. Pastor Dobias was very complimentary toward us. He said he noticed how hard I worked and that they had a great deal of respect for us and wanted to help us.

I knew there were some rooms in the basement and I also knew his study was located there, but what I didn't know was that there was also a rentable apartment in the basement. However, since Pastor Dobias needed a room for a study, he had decided not to rent it. He suggested that we rent it out, along with the upstairs apartment, and the income from these two apartments would exceed the house payments. This would mean that we would be paying the house off and basically living there for free.

What an offer! He said they knew we were young and that they just wanted to help us get ahead. Although I was ever so grateful for this opportunity, I really hated to see him leave. He was like a strong shepherd leading his flock.

After buying the house, we moved to the main floor. We had no trouble renting out the upstairs and basement apartments. I was really gung-ho now, as I was happy to start my new career as a painter.

191

I did a few more side jobs with Gary, but he had decided that he was working too much and wanted to spend more time with his family. I had become a workaholic and decided to push on without him. I do have some regrets about working too much and not spending more time with my boys as they were growing up.

Bill starting in business on
Field Avenue

I put an ad in the little shopper paper in our area. It was an effective means of advertising and everybody knew about it. My ad read: *Young painter desires more work. Small jobs a specialty.* I was surprised at the response. I loved small jobs. They were quick and I didn't have to wait for my money. I had many calls that would just involve one room or a stairwell. Gary had quit taking jobs but would work with me occasionally on my jobs. I managed to stay busy after work and on Sundays. I quickly moved up the ladder at work, and it wasn't long before I was making a higher hourly wage working for Charles Lawrence than I would have if I continued working at Quaker State Metal Products. I was kind of sad when I heard that they had gone out of business. I had met some nice people there and have only fond memories of that place.

Life was really good for us, and we could afford to travel around a lot. Most of our traveling amounted to going up to Ironwood and down to Mississippi. We probably visited both places about the same number of times. We continued being good friends with Glenda and Gary and Chuck.

Chuck had started dating a girl who lived in Milwaukee. They had met while they both attended a private high school called Wisconsin Academy. He introduced her to Edna and me, and later we went to Milwaukee to attend their wedding. I was happy for him. They bought a house just around the corner from us, and we had a long-lasting relationship with both of them. What a wonderful couple. Sharon, Chuck's wife, was a blast to be around. Her happy spirit was infectious as she smiled and laughed a lot. We loved our friends and our family.

My side workload continued to grow, and soon I was making more money after work than I was on my regular job. After working full time as a painter for only a year and a half, I decided to quit and go on my own. If I had counted my part-time work with Gary and the number of hours worked during my one-and-a-half-year tenure as a painter, it amounted to having approximately three years of full-time experience. I didn't want to quit my job. I really enjoyed it, but I was ready for a change. My workload continued to increase, and soon I had to hire a full-time painter to help me.

We were doing well enough that we were able to save the money to buy another new car. I liked my '64 Buick, but I was young and had the idea that a new car was a symbol of success. At the start of 1966 we bought a '66 Buick Special convertible. It was yellow with a black ragtop. Looking back now, this was probably my favorite car of all the ones I have owned.

Ted and Tim with 1966 Buick Special

Ted and Tim continued to grow and do well. I would make a point to always spend all the day and evening on Saturdays with them, even though I didn't spend much time with them through the week. My low self-esteem and total unhappiness had just about vanished at this point. I felt like the effort I had put out had come to fruition, and I was happy for myself and my family. My life had stabilized, and there was no way I could have possibly been any happier.

The only thing that remained, and that no amount of effort will ever erase, is the sadness I felt about the loss of my mother, which continues even to this day.

Ted and Bill having dinner at home
on Field Avenue

Ted, Edna, Tim — 1969

Bill — 1976

Tim — late 1990s

Tim, his wife Sue, and our
grandchildren Alex and Hannah
mid 1990s

19

Moving South

WE WERE VERY ACTIVE AS a married couple. I did a lot of work for the church with my responsibilities as Young People's Leader. We also spent as much time with our friends as possible. My schedule was very hectic, and there wasn't a lot of time for a social life, although we managed to slip it in somewhat.

Gary and Glenda had two girls who were close in age to our two boys. Almost every Saturday, we would have lunch together at one of our homes. Our full attention was turned to the children after lunch. We took them to the zoo, on nature hikes in the Forest Preserve, or to the lake. It was all about the kids after lunch until bedtime. We had a full life with a lot to be thankful for, but there was still something missing for Gary and Glenda, and it was missing for Edna and me also.

All four of us had grown up in the country. I was raised in Ironwood Township, Edna in northern Mississippi, Gary in the hills of Kentucky, and Glenda was from downstate Indiana. We all had a desire to get out of the Chicago area and the hustle and bustle of city life. There had been some race riots in nearby Maywood, Illinois, and that bothered us. Also, Ted was close to starting school, and we really wanted to get out of the big city before that happened. We did not have an immediate plan, but things evolved to the point where we were able to make the decision and move.

Gary still had relatives in Kentucky. His family had moved to Collegedale, Tennessee, when he was young, and this is where he had spent most of his school years. Collegedale was a small college town outside of Chattanooga, Tennessee. The town of Collegedale had two unincorporated areas, Apison and Ooltewah, that surrounded it. These were rural areas with a lot of open spaces.

In the latter part of 1966, Gary and Glenda decided to take another trip down there to visit some of their many friends. They had visited several times since we knew them, but this last trip was different. Gary went to see an old friend, Willard Watkins, who he had known growing up. Willard offered to sell Gary thirteen acres of land in Apison. The land was in Tennessee but bordered Georgia. As soon as he came back from the trip, he announced that he had bought thirteen acres in Apison, outside of Chattanooga.

My first question was, "What do you plan on doing with it?"

He replied, "We are thinking about moving there and building a new house on the property."

My heart sank. They were our best friends. Gary was like a brother to me, and Glenda and Edna were best friends. Now it sounded like we would be losing them.

He assured me that it would not happen right away because purchasing the property had drained him financially. They would have to stay, work, and save their money to be able to pull this off.

Gary took another trip by himself, just a short time later, to check on his property in relationship to building a house on it. He came back and realized that he needed more money than he had thought because he had to dig a well and put in a long driveway that went uphill quite a way.

He came straight over to talk to me and asked if I wanted to buy three acres of land from him. He said he really didn't need thirteen acres and that he needed the money more than the land.

I asked him, "How much do you want for the three acres?"

His answer shocked and surprised me when he said, "I will sell it to you for the same price that I paid for it — two hundred dollars an acre, which would be six hundred dollars for three acres."

My heart skipped a beat. I only had one other question and that was, "How does the land lay?"

His reply: "Slightly rolling, with a nice flat place to put a house."

That was it! I told him I would buy it sight unseen and gave him six hundred dollars. We would do the paperwork later. I bought it mostly because it was a good deal, and I didn't see how I could go wrong at that price. We did not have any intention of moving there to build a house on the property, at least not now.

After Gary purchased the property, he was "sitting on ready" as far as working as much as he could in order to save money to fulfill their plans of moving and building a house. Edna and I were not considering moving there at the time. Neither one of us had ever been to Tennessee and didn't really know if we would like it there.

We had considered moving to the South, but we weren't sure where. Mississippi was out of the question because of the vast rural area and poverty that existed there. I needed a larger population in order to be able to function in the painting business. I loved Iron wood, and still do, but that wouldn't work for some of the same reasons, and neither of us liked the very cold climate in the winter.

Gary picked up a few side jobs, but I was too busy to help him, so he did them himself. He also worked for me on the side whenever he could. I could not talk him into working for me full time because he felt a loyalty to Charles Lawrence, who really got him started in the painting business. He was paying Gary a good wage and treated him very well. Gary and Glenda were also renting from Charles Lawrence, who had given them a break on the rent because Gary worked for him.

Both Gary and Glenda wanted us to move to the South with them. We discussed it, but decided we were not ready to commit to moving at this time, even though our long-range plans were to get out of the city.

Early in 1967, Gary and Glenda decided to take another trip to Tennessee to plan the driveway needed for access to their property. Since the property did not have any road frontage, Willard Watkins had granted Gary a twelve-foot easement when he sold him the property. They invited Edna and I to go with them. We reasoned that since we owned three acres adjoining their property, and we had never even seen it, it would be good to travel there and look at the property.

That was it! We were smitten. Our acreage was beautiful with a gorgeous view. At the top of a hill, our property was straight ahead, while Gary and Glenda's was to the left. Therefore, the driveway would have to turn left at our property and go another fifty yards where Gary was planning to build their house. Our shared driveway ended at this point.

We spent several days in the area and Gary and I did a lot of driving around checking on the work situation. I was surprised how much building activity there was in the area. There were several subdivisions being built in the Ooltewah/Apison area, and quite a few near the Chattanooga city limits, about a twelve-mile drive from our property.

We realized that we could make this work. It was a difficult decision to give up my successful painting business in Broadview to move South and start all over. We reasoned that we would not be able to make much money to start with, but we felt like things would work out after we got established.

There were a couple of other pluses. If we built a house on our property, we would be living next door to Gary and Glenda, and we liked that idea. Gary also knew the area very well and had some good contacts. One of Gary's friends, David Jacobs, was living there and was a painter. Gary introduced us to David and his wife Betty. We liked them immediately. They were so humble and mannerly that it made a big impression on us.

The decision was made. I was going to give up my business, and we would sell the house and move to the Apison area, just outside of Chattanooga. This decision was probably made in the spring of 1967, and we were getting excited and also a little nervous.

I had some confidence that I could go down South and get into the painting business; however, there was some concern about taking this huge leap of faith. We felt this move would be the best thing to do for our family. Ted had turned six years old, but we had already decided to hold him out of kindergarten and start him in first grade. We would wait until 1968 to enroll Ted in first grade at Spalding Elementary, a private school located on the campus of Southern Missionary College. He would turn seven years old a month after school started.

This was like a dream many people have of building a house in the country and owning some acreage to go with it, as opposed to living in the city with all of the houses crammed together. We were caught up in this mentality, and now we were ready to take action. We had lot to do as we contemplated building our new house.

The first thing I did was put our house on the market in the fall of 1967. We couldn't go anywhere until we sold our house. The house sold in early November, and we closed around the third week of the month. Our goal was to get everything ready so that we could hit the road as soon as we closed on the house and got our money.

I had several months of work scheduled. I talked to the two men who worked for me and asked if they would like to do the jobs and keep the money because I would be moving. They agreed. I explained everything to my customers, which cleared the way for my men to do the work without my involvement.

I also had a ledger of everyone I worked for that included their addresses and phone numbers. I sent them all a letter informing them that I was going out of business. I enclosed the name and phone number of Roger Carlson, who was one of my painters, and suggested they call him if they needed any work done in the future. I parted on good terms with both men, and they did quite well down the road.

Gary and Glenda decided to rent a house in Collegedale, about six miles from where they were going to build their house. They figured they would move on down ahead of us, get their furniture set up in their house, and then return to help us move.

The problem was that we had more vehicles than drivers. In order for Gary and Glenda to help us, they needed to leave their vehicles at home, and come and drive one of our vehicles. They were able to catch a ride with someone who lived in Collegedale and needed to come to the Chicago area. Their children were still in Broadview staying with Glenda's mother. They would be reunited with their parents when we hit the road for Tennessee.

The plan was working quite well. I had purchased an old 1954 Diamond T truck to move our belongings. I knew that trucks sold for more in the South than they did in the North. I thought I could buy this old truck to move our furniture to Tennessee and then sell the truck for a profit. How clever is that?! I had figured that we would actually make money on this move. Wrong! This decision turned out to be a disaster. Also, part of our plan was to live with Gary and Glenda just long enough for us to find a house to rent while we were preparing to build a new house.

We closed on the house and came away with about six thousand dollars, which was a real blessing because we did not put any money down on the house, and the rent was more than ample to make the payment. I cannot say enough kind words about Pastor

Dobias and express my heartfelt thanks to him for making this all possible. We had managed to save some money, and I sold most of my equipment. So, at least we were not moving to the South broke.

Gary and I packed the old Diamond T full of stuff. We thought we knew what we were doing (we didn't) by using blankets and tying some things with rope. So here we go in a caravan headed South, with all our money and material possessions, plus four children. It was a complete break from the North.

Edna just before
we moved South

They had a big farewell dinner at the church, and there were some tears shed that night. I had sold the 1955 Chevy and replaced it with a 1960 Ford station wagon. It was pretty well loaded with my painting tools and even some ladders tied on top. Then we had our 1966 Buick convertible to drive. It started out with Gary driving the Diamond T with Glenda in front with him. I was driving my Ford station wagon and Edna was driving the Buick with three of the children in it.

Ted started out riding with me. We did swap places quite a bit on the trip, with one exception. Gary loved driving that old truck, and I certainly did not have any objections to that, so he was the only driver of the truck. Sometimes Glenda would drive my station wagon with one of her children in the front seat and I would ride with Gary. It was mostly Gary and I in the truck after the initial start of the trip. Glenda and Edna swapped places a few times as it was a little hectic with three small children in the Buick. This trip wound up being an adventure. It was around Thanksgiving of 1967, and I was twenty-five years old.

When I originally came up with the brilliant, but not too smart, idea to buy an older cheap truck to move us from Broadview to Tennessee, I started searching everywhere. My idea was that it didn't have to be that good, as long as it would get us there. When I found the 1954 Diamond T, it did have some mechanical problems. But Chuck, who was with me when I found it, suggested that his friend, Norm, take a look at it and estimate how much it would cost to do the necessary repair.

Norm was a good mechanic who had a shop in Broadview. I had already bought the truck so it was not contingent upon his evaluation. I wanted the repairs done before we left and wanted some idea as to the cost of the repairs. When he told us everything that was wrong with it and how much it would cost to fix it, I felt the price was reasonable and told him to go ahead. When we picked up the truck and took it to our house, it was running fine. It seemed to run well starting out, but it was like it had a governor on it. We could not get it to go faster than fifty-five miles an hour.

Gary had come up with the brainstorm of going over the mountains in Kentucky to a little town called Stearns to visit his grandmother. He had told me a lot about his grandmother and that she basically had raised him. He loved her very much and wanted us to meet her. He also had an uncle and a few cousins who lived there.

I was okay with that because we were in no hurry. We didn't have a job yet, so we might as well take our time and enjoy the mountains. Anyway, that sounded good.

The problem was that the Diamond T did not like the mountains at all. The truck would moan and groan as we seemed to barely top some of the hills. We would try to get a good head of steam to climb the mountains, but the truck would go slower and slower, and we were going around fifteen miles an hour before we started down.

Finally, on one of the mountains, it stopped running. Fortunately there was a place to pull off the road. It was like someone turned the key off. It would not start again. Now we were really in a

Family visit to Mammoth Cave in Kentucky — 1967

201

pickle. We were still a long way from Stearns. The only thing we knew to do was sit there until someone came along, hopefully a police officer, and arrange to have our truck towed somewhere.

Edna and Glenda had pulled over and were behind us trying to motion us to keep going. *Yeah, right!* That truck was not going to move. I couldn't figure out where my cell phone was. Okay, now I remember, we didn't have cell phones back then. *Ha-ha!* That sure would have helped.

Finally, a Kentucky State Trooper came along and he was very nice about the situation as he realized that we were two families with children and we were stranded. Gary and I had thought earlier about sending Edna and Glenda ahead to see if they could find a garage that had a tow truck, but since none of us knew how far or where that would be, we decided to just sit still.

The officer radioed ahead and made arrangements for a tow truck to come and get the truck. He told us he would stay with the truck and that we could go on. He also gave us directions to the nearest motel because it was getting dark. He then informed us that it would probably be the next day before a mechanic would be able to work on it, so he wrote their phone number on a piece of paper and advised me to call them when we got up in the morning.

Our original plan was to make it to Stearns by nightfall where Gary's grandmother had arranged for us to spend the night. Okay, so scrap that idea. We didn't make it.

At this point I started regretting not having a moving company move us. If I would have done that, we wouldn't have had to pay a motel bill for four adults and four children. I certainly felt obligated to pay for everyone since Gary and Glenda were doing us a favor by helping us move. Gary offered to pay for his family, but I would not hear of it. It was my decision making that got us into this mess.

I called the garage in the morning to see about the truck. They had just started checking it out and told me to call back in about an hour. I did, and they had diagnosed the problem and were working on it. They estimated they would probably be finished around lunchtime. So, we picked up the truck and got back on the road again. Gary had called his grandmother and told her we were still coming, but we were a day behind schedule.

When we finally got to Stearns, it was mid to late afternoon and we decided to spend some time visiting with everyone, stay the night there, and leave early in the morning. Gary's grandmother fixed us a very nice supper and we were all thankful. As part of our sleeping arrangements, Edna and I and the boys would be staying at Gary's uncle's house, while Gary, Glenda, and the girls would be staying with Grandma. His uncle had eaten supper with us and was very cordial. We felt comfortable going to his house to spend the night. In the morning, we met back at Gary's grandmother's house and had a great breakfast before hitting the road again.

The old Diamond T kept chugging along, but it seemed to be getting slower and slower. I am not sure if part of the problem was that we were overloaded and putting too much strain on the motor, or if old age had taken its toll. I did know the truck was old and worn out, but hey, we were making it.

About twenty miles before we got to Gary and Glenda's house, we noticed the engine on the Diamond T was smoking. We were just hoping and praying that it didn't blow up before we got there. It didn't!

We finally arrived at his house and parked the truck in his yard. We felt so relieved. Since our first order of business was to find a house to rent, we just left the truck packed the way it was. At least we did have the foresight to pack all our clothes in the car and the station wagon. We were all pretty exhausted by now, and it was nice to go to bed early.

It wasn't long before Edna and I found a house to rent. It was also in Collegedale, only two or three miles from Gary and Glenda's house. Fortunately, the driveway and the yard were big enough to park the old Diamond T. Gary and I took everything out of the truck and set up our house. We left the truck sitting there empty and figured that we could use it one more time when we built our new house. At least we hoped for that. After we got to working, I ended up using the truck for a storage shed.

Now it was time to focus on finding work and building our house on the three acres that we had in Apison. The old Diamond T had one more huge surprise for us, and it wasn't very pleasant.

We were now in our rental house in Collegedale and in the process of lining up the building of our new house in Apison. Gary's childhood friend, Fred Edgmon,

Edna, Ted at Apison property — 1968

was active in the house-building trade but worked for his father, Lee, who was a house builder. Fred was a hard worker and did a lot of the work on the houses his dad built. He had worked for his father long enough that he knew the building trade and was hankering to go into business for himself. They had recently completed a new home in Collegedale, and he took all of us to see it. It was a tri-level home that was very popular in the late '60s. In fact, most of the houses we worked on were either tri-levels or split foyers.

We all loved the house, and Gary, Glenda, Edna, and I sat down to talk about our new homes. We were confident that Fred knew what he was doing, and we decided to ask him to build both of our houses. He jumped at the chance because this would be the inauguration of his career as a home builder. These two houses would be the first that Fred had ever built on his own.

Fred's career took off from that point, and Gary and I were proud to say that ours were the first houses that Fred Edgmon built. He became a very successful builder for many years. Then he went into developing subdivisions and became very well-known in our area as a developer. He was one of those unforgettable characters that most of us meet during our lifetime. He always had a smile and seemed to be a very happy person, and was fun to be around.

I can't help but think of the bathrooms in homes and how they have developed over the years. Most of the middle-class houses built in the '50s, and even into the '60s, had only one bathroom. I thought it was great to have a bathroom inside of the house — period. Having two bathrooms in a house was a luxury that most people did not have.

Home building had developed to the point where houses were being built with one and a half bathrooms, with the half bath in the master bedroom. We really thought we were uptown now, since our new house was going to have two commodes. We had never had more than one bathroom before and we were excited about having a bathroom in our bedroom. Wow! Imagine that! We were going to have two bathrooms inside of the house. Life couldn't get any better than that!

We made our decision to build the exact house Fred had shown us. Gary had decided the same thing. Our houses would be identical except for the color of the exterior, carpets, and appliances.

Most of the houses being built in our area did not have central air conditioning and heat. We had ceiling heat and four air conditioners installed in the walls — one each in the kitchen-dining area, living room, master bedroom, and family room, located on the lower level. They did the job and kept us warm in the winter and cool in the summer.

The three bedrooms and both bathrooms were on the top floor. On the middle floor were the living room and kitchen-dining combination. The family and laundry rooms were on the lower level. The house had a total of 1,540 square feet of living area.

This was during the time when avocado green and harvest gold colors were popular. If you had avocado green appliances, then you had harvest gold carpet, which is what we had. Gary and Glenda reversed this in their house by getting harvest gold appliances and avocado green carpet.

Fred had given us a "lock and key" price on both of our houses. He charged us ten dollars per square foot for everything. Think about that: it amounted to $15,400, lock, stock, and barrel. Since I had paid six hundred dollars for our three acres and split the cost of the road and of digging the well with Gary, I had a little over $17,000 in the whole project. We put a down payment of $4,000 on the house and financed the balance with a bank. Okay, are you ready for this? Our house payments, which included taxes and insurance, were $111 per month.

Think how neat it would be if we could bring back the prices of the late '60s with the money we are making now. Hmmm! A house back then was a lot cheaper than most cars are now. Oh well, everything is relative as long as wages keep up with inflation.

Fred started on our houses around March of 1968. He worked hard and pushed both of our houses through to completion in four months. We were ready to move into them in late July 1968. When Fred completed our house, he called us and asked us to do a walk-through, and if we saw something we were not happy with, he would fix it before we moved in. Neither of us could find anything wrong even though we tried our best to be thorough.

When Fred left, the kids were playing in the yard and we both stood there and looked at each other. Our new house was ready to move into. I asked Edna, "What do you think about it?"

She made eye contact with me and started to cry. This got to me enough that I felt something warm running down my cheek also. We held hands and knelt down on the living room carpet and thanked God for this tremendous gift that He had bestowed on us.

I felt so unworthy. Thoughts of my childhood came rushing back into my mind, and the prayers that I used to say, asking God to be with me through the very hard times I was going through. I also thought of all the children who were now living in the same conditions that I had to live through. It was hard for me to realize that I had come from total poverty to owning my own brand-new home.

Now, it was time to move. We pulled the old Diamond T out of retirement, and Gary and Glenda came over and we packed everything into it, hoping it would make it to our new house. I was especially worried about the truck making it up the hill to our house because it had started smoking before we got to Chattanooga.

Well, folks, I did not have to worry about the truck making it up the hill as it turned out. It was probably about six miles or so to our house. Gary and I jumped in the truck and Glenda and Edna and the kids all piled in the car. We got about half way there and heard this loud *blam!* That was it. The Diamond T died, never to rise again.

Bummer! Now what were we going to do? Here we were standing on a country road alongside a truck that had all our belongings in it, and it would not run. Gary came up with the solution. He knew somebody nearby who had a pickup, so we left Glenda, Edna, and the children there and Gary and I got in the car and headed over to his friend's house. His name was Billy Watkins, and he was the son of Willard Watkins, who Gary had bought the land from. He was very cordial and not only loaned us his pickup, but jumped in to help us.

Fortunately, we were able to guide the old truck far enough off the road when it blew up so that it would not be a problem. We suggested that Edna, Glenda, and the kids go to the house ahead of us. I don't remember how many loads it took, but we unloaded the old truck and moved everything to the house and left the truck sitting on the side of the road. Fortunately, we had started this move fairly early in the morning and we were able to accomplish this before dark.

I ended up selling the Diamond T to the man who owned the gas station where I bought my gas. I told him that if he gave me a tank of gas and went and picked up the truck, he could have it. That was the end of the old 1954 Diamond T.

20
Adjusting to Southern Living

IT WAS HARD TO BELIEVE that we had moved to a strange place in the South where we did not know our way around, we had plans to build a new house, and I didn't even have a job. This was a challenge, but I felt comfortable that I would be able to find work and get rolling. I also knew that I would have to make a major adjustment in how I did business.

There was a huge difference between Chattanooga and Chicago. There were three or four million people in the Chicago area, many of whom were affluent. Not so in the Chattanooga area with its population of approximately two hundred thousand. There were affluent people, but not as many because of the smaller population.

In the painting trade and also in other trades, there are two types of work, redo/remodel work and new construction. Up to this point, I had done residential and light commercial repaint work, and in most cases I worked directly for homeowners. I had no interest in doing new construction work in the Chicago area for a couple of reasons. One was that there wasn't as much money in new work, unless you were equipped with a lot of spray equipment and had multiple crews of men. There was also the problem with labor unions. They had all the new work tied up, and it wasn't smart to attempt to do any new work. I never had trouble with the unions because I stayed away from their turf.

Now we were in a completely different work environment. Tennessee is a "right to work" state, and you could do new work without joining the union. I quickly realized that it would take far too long to build up a residential repaint business here because of the smaller population. There was a lot of new home construction going on and we could get a volume of work by getting into that, even though there wasn't as much money in it. I knew the repaint market would come over time.

Gary was a great asset because he knew people, and he knew the area really well. We had decided not to look for work until we settled in. We all drove around for a few days, went out to our property a couple of times, and hung out for a week or so.

After that first week, it was time to get serious about our work situation. The first thing Gary and I decided to do was to visit his friend David Jacobs and his wife, Betty. David was working full time as a painter in the area, and we wanted his thoughts on how to proceed in finding work.

David was working for Milton Larcum, a paint contractor who I later got to know really well. David had been approached, just a day or two before we talked to him, by some builders who had asked if he wanted to paint a couple of new houses that would be ready in a week or so. David had told them he would like to, but that it would be too much work to do by himself.

I jumped on that and asked David if he would be willing to do the houses if Gary and I worked with him. I suggested that we split the money three ways. This seemed fair because I had most of the tools and equipment and Gary had a lot of paint brushes. I also

David Jacobs and Bill holding checks collected in 1968

suggested to David that we take him in as a third partner, and I would hustle up work to keep us busy. He liked the idea and quit his job with Milton Larcum.

We were off and running, but we only had these two new houses to paint, inside and out. David had taken a chance by quitting his full-time job to work with us. We weren't established here, but he told me later that it was a gut feeling, and he just went with it.

I was now twenty-five years old and realized that I had to shift into high gear. I was in relentless pursuit of new houses. Things were much different back then as opposed to now. When we started out, developers would start a subdivision by purchasing the property, surveying it for building lots, and putting in the roads. They stayed out of the construction end of it. They made their money by selling the lots to builders, and there were many builders back then. There were subdivisions being developed all over the outskirts of the city, and I was after the work.

I had talked to David and Gary and asked if they would work on those two houses by themselves, and I would drive around town talking to builders and try to drum up work. They agreed, and there I went. I drove to every subdivision I could find and started talking to the builders if I could catch them on the job. I would talk to them as long as they wanted. I was honest and told them we had moved down here and were trying to get established. I told them we would do a good job and we would see the job through from start to finish without pulling off to do another job. Then I would hand them a business card. If the builder was not on the job, I would get his name and phone number from their sign — they all had signs — and call them at night.

During this time, there were no cell phones, and all of the calls had to be done after supper when people were at home. There was no such thing as calling a builder during the day. I remember having a list of around twenty-five builders, and I would spend many evenings on the phone talking to them. I devoted one entire week to doing this. It was day and night, Monday through Friday, and it paid off. I picked up two more houses during this same week with many more to come from my initial contacts. Many builders didn't want to commit until it was close to being time to have the painting done. I knew the only way we were going to be successful was that we had to have a volume of work, split up, and the three of us would each lead a crew of four painters. We were starting to roll and were knocking out the jobs.

It was March of 1968. Even though I was not making near the money I made in Chicago, we were making a living and I knew it would get much better as we became established and started working for homeowners. I felt good about the fact that I had moved to a new city and started a new business, with fifteen people involved, in just four months.

During this same time, I put advertisements in the newspaper and later took out a yellow page ad. From the time I went into business for myself in Broadview to this very day, I never had to work for anyone else.

Bill, Edna, Angela, Tim, Ted
1976

Tim, Angela, Ted — 1978

I am ever so thankful to God who heard my prayers way back when I was a poverty-stricken youngster growing up in Ironwood Township. I was now realizing that He had a hand in all of this.

My primary reason for writing this book, as mentioned earlier, was to portray my childhood through my eyes as a child when I was going through difficult times. Research has proven, beyond the shadow of a doubt, that conditional, psychological, physical, and mental abuse during childhood is a contributing factor to the onset of mental illness, addiction, and self-destructive behavior later in life.

I mentioned in the Introduction that to be successful the opportunity is there, just waiting for hard-working, dedicated people to find it. I did not mention the flip side that there are many pitfalls where people will make bad choices, and their conduct and association with the wrong people will also have a negative influence on them. There is a world of crime, drugs, and alcohol just waiting for all those who make bad choices. Sometimes it seems the way to go because it can help to cover up the pain to a certain extent, but the problem is that it never leads to happiness and is only a temporary fix with devastating effects on their lives to follow.

The solution for ending pain that comes from a traumatized childhood will never come from a temporary fix, but rather from a resolve, that is God-given, to be willing to make good decisions, putting unhappiness on the side, and finding positive people in your life with a determination to make them happy. At that point happiness will automatically follow as you feel your self-worth rise quickly. In listing some of my accomplishments later in life, I only do so to illustrate that it is possible to achieve a good quality of life and be happy even though life appears dark when you are staggering under the weight of a very unhappy childhood.

I would like to condense the rest of my story in the form of a summary. We lived in our new house in Apison for about five years before moving to the other side of Chattanooga to another new house we built. To sum it up, we lived in five new homes, including the one we are in now. My painting business flourished through the years, and I also added a wash business called Miracle Wash to the services we offered. Later, we added vinyl siding. Then we got a state contractor's license and added remodeling and building to our repertoire. There was a time when I had thirty-five employees, including four full-time carpenters, but through it all, the painting business was always my main thrust.

I was also heavily into real estate. At one point I had six duplexes and four houses that I rented. I bought and sold well over one hundred houses in my lifetime.

I opened, sold, or closed four different restaurants. One was called Fifth Avenue Yogurt. It was during the yogurt craze that was gathering steam, but ended up falling flat as we soon learned it was just a fad. I hired a manager to run this store as I did not have the time because of my other profitable businesses. We kept it open for about one and a half years before closing it because we were breaking even at best.

Next, I bought The Country Churn. It was primarily an ice cream store with over forty varieties of ice cream. We served breakfast to order, and at lunch we served hamburgers and sandwiches with a small salad bar. Edna liked this shop when we looked at it and decided that she would run it, since she had some restaurant experience. We inherited the staff from the previous owners, so we were ready to go. The previous owner consented to remain with us for two weeks to help us get oriented.

Edna, Bill at The Country Churn restaurant — early 1980s

211

Bill, Edna at Billy-Bobs pizza
tavern — mid-1980s

We were in a strip center, and the person renting the suite next to us went out of business. That is when I decided to rent it and put in a pizza place. We called it Billy-Bobs. We also served beer and, as time went on, it became more of a tavern than a family pizza place.

Edna was getting tired of the grind of running The Country Churn and felt she needed to spend more time with our daughter, Angela. I cut an opening in the wall, closed The Country Churn, and added this space to Billy-Bobs for pool tables and dart boards. The business was doing okay financially, but I was spending too much time there with my friends. It was taking from the time I should have spent on my more profitable construction companies. So, I let the final lease run out, sold all the equipment, and shut it down.

Later I opened a business in East Ridge, Tennessee, called Skewers Deli. I had met a man who had been in the restaurant business and specialized in a very popular sandwich in this area called "Steak in a Sack." That got me into financing the opening of the store. He ran it, and we would split the profit. This turned out to be a disaster. I will not go into detail, but we ended up selling the

Tim, Bill, Ted, Baby Angela
1975

business. I was fortunate not to lose very much money. Yes, I had my fill of the food business and never again attempted getting involved in another restaurant.

Another big highlight in our life was when our daughter, Angela, was born on February 26, 1975. We called her our caboose baby because she was ten years younger than our youngest son, Tim. Imagine having a baby girl ten years after having two boys. Our family was complete.

One of the enjoyable things we were able to do happened in July of 1985. Edna and I vacationed in Hawaii for a couple of weeks to celebrate our twenty-fifth anniversary. We attended the Don Ho show, which was a big production dinner show with dancers. Edna treasures a picture of herself with Don Ho after the show. I think the only hit song that he ever had was "Tiny Bubbles," but his show was outstanding and seemed to be on everyone's bucket list who went to Hawaii on vacation.

Arrival in Hawaii — 1985

Life has been a great ride to this point, and I am so thankful for what I have accomplished during my lifetime. I believe the hardships I suffered in my early childhood were God's way of honing and preparing me for adulthood. I have never taken anything for granted and realize I would not have been able to accomplish anything without the gift of health and strength that comes from our Creator. I am also grateful to God for hearing my prayers, as I cried out to Him so very often in my youth when I felt all alone in this world and destined for a life of unhappiness.

Edna with Don Ho

Edna and Bill at a luau

Because of my childhood years, my heart goes out to the young people who are struggling at home. To those of you who have lost a parent, to those of you who are being raised with an abusive alcoholic parent, and also to those of you who are living in poverty and struggling with low self-esteem, be of good cheer, because the Master is near. Your pain and suffering does not go unnoticed, and you are not alone. You may not be able to do anything about your situation now, but rest assured, your day and time is coming and you will have opportunities to emerge from the pain and suffering that you are feeling.

I would like to acknowledge you, dear reader, for supporting me as I tried my best to provide an overview of my life with the hope that my story will be an inspiration to someone who is involved in an unhappy home life. If this turns out to be the case, I will feel that the energy I put forth in writing this book will be well worth the effort.

Angela — 1977

Angela — 1981

Our family — Ted, Bill, Angela, Tim, Edna — 2000

Acknowledgements

I REALIZE THAT I AM departing from what is considered the normal standard procedure in writing a book. I could not bring this book to a close without paying tribute to the three people who were instrumental for me being able to begin this book and bring it to fruition. They are Alvar Helmes, Joanne Verbos Brown, and Lois Matson. They have been by my side the entire time bringing advice, encouragement, and good work ethics to the mix. I believe it was more than coincidence that the four of us came together in this joint effort. Through the power of the Internet, we were able to form a team with a common bond. We are all from the Upper Peninsula of Michigan. Yes! We are all Yoopers.

Alvar Helmes and I met by being members of the "You Know You Are From Ironwood When..." Facebook group. Alvar and I went to the same high school, Luther L. Wright, in Ironwood, Michigan, but he graduated before I started there and I never had the opportunity to meet him in person. Our connection began when he expressed interest in some of my

writings that were posted in the Ironwood group. Alvar brought his expertise in editing to this project, and I will forever be grateful for the wisdom and leadership that he provided in that role.

Alvar has worked in the publications field for much of his adult life. His longest term-writing job was with Honeywell, Inc., Minneapolis, Minnesota, as a technical writer.

He was born in Iron Belt, Wisconsin, the youngest of ten children. When Alvar was six years old, his father died at the age of fifty-two from silicosis due to breathing the silica dust in the iron ore mines. When he was ten years old, the family moved to Ironwood, Michigan, to take advantage of better schooling and more job opportunities. Alvar lived in Ironwood for eight years and graduated from Luther L. Wright High School. After a three-year stint in the Army, he returned to Ironwood and completed one year at Gogebic Junior College. Shortly thereafter, he married a local girl, Nancy Hannu.

He and his wife had eight children (five boys and three girls), and were married for fifty-five years before his wife passed away in 2006. He lives in Battle Ground, Washington, and is still actively involved in publications work. In 2002 he and his family established a Mission Hospital in India. Most of his writing is concerned with literature needed for maintaining the activities of the hospital.

 I met Joanne Verbos Brown in the same way that I met Alvar, but we did have more in common. Joanne went to Roosevelt School, as I did, except she was a couple of years behind me and I never got to know her then. We had the same teachers at Roosevelt and at Luther L. Wright. That gave us good topics for conversation later.

One of the neatest things was the fact that my dad, John Spetz, and her dad, Joe Verbos, were both loggers in Upper Michigan at the same time. They knew each other and worked together at times. When Joanne asked me if I knew him, I replied that I vaguely knew of a Joe Verbos. That sparked an instant bond.

Joanne grew up with her parents and three brothers in Ironwood Township. She graduated from Luther L. Wright with the class of 1962. Following her graduation, she became a Wisconsin resident when the Verbos family relocated to Kenosha. She began her career at S.C. Johnson in Racine, then Case Corporation and Abbott Laboratories. She is currently in real estate. Joanne earned her B.A. in Business and Communication from Concordia University-Wisconsin. She attained her Certified Purchasing Manager status as well as her Realtor license and is an Accredited Staging Professional.

Joanne has two married sons and five grandchildren who are her heart's delight. She has always had an adventurous spirit and enjoys traveling in the United States and internationally where her priority is to absorb local cultures, meet new friends, walk beaches, and shop for treasures.

When I first began posting on Facebook, she found my story compelling and she understood the Upper Peninsula lifestyle. I contacted her thinking she was an English teacher and asked her if she would be interested in helping with my book. Although she wasn't an English major, her early years as an Executive Secretary prepared her for this task.

Lois Matson and I became acquainted through Alvar. She and Alvar often have worked together on projects that they have in common.

Lois was born below the bridge in Detroit, Michigan, but was raised in the Upper Peninsula from the age of two. She attended Chassell Township Schools for most of her academic years and married at the young age of seventeen and moved from Michigan.

She and her husband, Al, have raised eight children in the Pacific Northwest, living there for over thirty years. She is the proud grammy of six, soon to be seven, grandchildren. Lois is a life-long learner and teacher. Her most recent interests are theology and computer coding. Technology fascinates her, and she has a deep love for words. Language is a powerful medium for communication; so well-written phrases, sentences, and paragraphs delight her. Music, especially sacred music, holds a special place in her heart. Lois has long been involved as editor, contributor, and designer for various church and ministry publications.

About the Author

William Theodore Payne (Bill) has been a business contractor in Chattanooga, Tennessee, for most of his adult life. His primary thrust has been in the painting trade, but he has also dealt heavily in real estate ventures that include building, remodeling, and selling houses. He lives with his wife of fifty-nine years, Edna, and their dog Tinkerbell. His adult children — Ted, Tim, and Angie — also live in Chattanooga.

Bill spent his formative years in Ironwood, a small city on the western end of the Upper Peninsula of Michigan. His love for this area runs deep, and he still considers it home.

The drama, sadness, and total poverty that Bill experienced because of a broken home have given him the inspiration to write his life story. Hopefully, it will encourage others who have had similar experiences to press on and to not give up hope for a better life.

If you have any questions or comments, feel free to contact Bill at: William Payne, P.O. Box 21225, Chattanooga, TN 37424.

Made in the USA
Columbia, SC
14 April 2021